REAL ESTATE

ESTATE

— RULES —

REAL ESTATE
—RULES—

The INVESTOR'S GUIDE *to*

PICKING **WINNERS** *and*

AVOIDING **LOSERS**

in LISTED PROPERTY

HARM MEIJER

WILEY

This edition first published 2025.

© 2025 Harm Meijer

All rights reserved. No part of this publication may be reproduced, stored in a retrieval system, or transmitted, in any form or by any means, electronic, mechanical, photocopying, recording or otherwise, except as permitted by law. Advice on how to obtain permission to reuse material from this title is available at http://www.wiley.com/go/permissions.

The right of Harm Meijer to be identified as the authors of this work has been asserted in accordance with law.

Registered Offices
John Wiley & Sons, Inc., 111 River Street, Hoboken, NJ 07030, USA
John Wiley & Sons Ltd, New Era House, 8 Oldlands Way, Bognor Regis, West Sussex, PO22 9NQ, UK

For details of our global editorial offices, customer services, and more information about Wiley products visit us at www.wiley.com.

Wiley also publishes its books in a variety of electronic formats and by print-on-demand. Some content that appears in standard print versions of this book may not be available in other formats.

Trademarks: Wiley and the Wiley logo are trademarks or registered trademarks of John Wiley & Sons, Inc. and/or its affiliates in the United States and other countries and may not be used without written permission. All other trademarks are the property of their respective owners. John Wiley & Sons, Inc. is not associated with any product or vendor mentioned in this book.

Limit of Liability/Disclaimer of Warranty

While the publisher and authors have used their best efforts in preparing this work, they make no representations or warranties with respect to the accuracy or completeness of the contents of this work and specifically disclaim all warranties, including without limitation any implied warranties of merchantability or fitness for a particular purpose. No warranty may be created or extended by sales representatives, written sales materials or promotional statements for this work. This work is sold with the understanding that the publisher is not engaged in rendering professional services. The advice and strategies contained herein may not be suitable for your situation. You should consult with a specialist where appropriate. The fact that an organization, website, or product is referred to in this work as a citation and/or potential source of further information does not mean that the publisher and authors endorse the information or services the organization, website, or product may provide or recommendations it may make. Further, readers should be aware that websites listed in this work may have changed or disappeared between when this work was written and when it is read. Neither the publisher nor authors shall be liable for any loss of profit or any other commercial damages, including but not limited to special, incidental, consequential, or other damages.

Library of Congress Cataloging-in-Publication Data is Available:

ISBN 9781394324859 (Cloth)
ISBN 9781394324866 (ePub)
ISBN 9781394324873 (ePDF)

Cover Design: Wiley
Cover Images: © FourLeafLover/Adobe Stock, © Zhaidar/Adobe Stock

Set in 11.5/14pt BemboStd by Straive, Chennai, India
SKY10097983_020625

Life is about learning and overcoming hurdles with a positive mind. The day you stop learning, you have become old.

Contents

Foreword	xiii
Preface	xix
Introduction – A Sector Not to Be Ignored	1
Real Estate Is an Important Asset Class	1
Two Undesirable Features of Real Estate	5
Listed Real Estate Has Attractive Features	6
But Listed Real Estate Is Not Always Preferred (Although It Should Be!)	8
Listed Real Estate Is a Great Hunting Ground and Poised for Growth	9
Book Organisation	11
Notes	12
The 20 Golden Rules of Real Estate	13
Part I Real Estate	15
Chapter 1 High Yield for a Reason	17
How Is the Yield Exactly Calculated?	
Is It 'Dressed Up'?	18
Is It a Good Asset?	19

vii

Chapter 2	Look for a Rent Compounding Machine with Minimum Capex	21
	Real Estate with Strong Supply/Demand Dynamics	22
	Ability to Capture Rental Growth Potential	29
	Minimum Capital Expenditure and Incentives	33
Chapter 3	Scan for Value Add Potential	35
	Refurbishment, Extension and Alternative Use	35
	Cluster or Platform Creation	36
	Development	36
	Acquisitions and Disposals	37
	Services	37
Chapter 4	Real Estate Is Cyclical	39
	Warning Signs	40
	Taking the Contrarian Side	44
	Note	45
Chapter 5	Expected Returns Should Beat Cost of Capital	47
	Yield and Price per Square Metre	48
	Expected Return	48
	Beat the Cost of Capital	49
	Conservative Underwriting	51
	Act!	52
Chapter 6	Central Bank and Government Stimuli (or Lack of) Can Be Game Changers	55
	Central Banks Tend to Get Their Way	58
	Engineered Volatility, but …	58
	Bail Out if 'Majority Is in Trouble'	59
	Stimulus or Restrictive Policy Will End One Day	59
	Arbitrage Opportunities Opening Up	59
Part II	Capital Structure	61
Chapter 7	Prudent Use of Financial Leverage: Don't Get Caught Out by Downturns	63
	Capital Markets Do Not Reward High Leverage, the Opposite!	64

Contents		ix

	Loose or No Covenants	65
	Can Absorb a Value Decline of at Least 40%	65
	No Endless Leverage on Valuation Gains	66
	Increasingly Difficult to Degear above 50% LTV	67
	Note	69
Chapter 8	Don't Assume That Financing Will Always Be Available	71
	Sufficient Cash Flow	72
	Spread in Maturities and Lenders	72
	Equity Should Be Raised When Conditions Are Favourable	72
	Alternative Financing	73
	Good Relationships with Debt Providers	73
	Rights Issues Value Destructive in Downturns	74
	Notes	78
Part III	Management	79
Chapter 9	Continuous Value Creation Is Key	81
	Value Creation Leads to Superior Shareholder Value	81
	Optimising Total Returns from the Real Estate (ROIC)	83
	Optimising the Capital Structure (WACC)	84
	Cœur Défense – An Example of Strong Value Creation	85
	M&A Can Add Value, But Frequently It Has Not	90
	Notes	97
Chapter 10	Radical Action Needed in Case of Shareholder Value Destruction	99
	Change Management, Board and/or Governance	100
	Return of Capital	100
	Circle Property Trust: Liquidating Itself	101
Chapter 11	Overconfidence Leads to Downfall	103
	Capital & Regional – The Remarkable Example of Overconfidence	104

Chapter 12	Corporate Governance Should Be Top Nudge	107
	Risk Management	109
	Transparency	110
	Governance Dynamics	110
	Remuneration	111
	Compounding Goodwill	115
Part IV	Investing in Listed Real Estate	117
Chapter 13	Scrutinise Property Investment Vehicles	119
	First Impressions Can Be Misleading	119
	Focus on Cash Flow	122
	Mosaic Theory	125
	Notes	126
Chapter 14	Significant Upside Based on Multicriteria Valuations	127
	Historical Performance Analysis	127
	Six Basic Valuation Metrics	128
	Modelling	131
	Invest with Margin for Error	134
Chapter 15	Focus on (Upcoming) Value Creators, Be Careful with Destroyers	137
	Introducing a Framework: Get on the Right Highway!	138
	(a) Firing on All Cylinders	139
	(b) Potentials	144
	(c) Stuck	144
	(d) Fighting for Survival	146
	The Accelerator Effect	147
	Note	150
Chapter 16	Look for Maximum Pessimism and Maximum Optimism	151
Chapter 17	Ensure Management, the Board and Other Shareholders Are Aligned with Investment Objectives	155

	Contents	xi

	Management and Board Alignment	156
	Investigate the Shareholder Base	159
	Note	160
Chapter 18	Be Aware of Self-Liquidating Companies	161
	Unsustainable Dividends	161
	Sustainable Dividend Policy	162
	intu Properties Plc – In Denial	163
Chapter 19	When Trust Is Gone, There Is No Limit to Downside	177
	Spotting Red Flags	177
	The Downfall of SBB	178
	Adler Group: Everything That Possibly Could Go Wrong Went Wrong	181
	Note	192
Chapter 20	Understand the Stock Market (Rules)	193
	Have a Conviction, Listen to the Models	193
	Be Proactive	194
	Analysts Not Good at Spotting 'Turning' Points	194
	When Management Teams Are Upset ...	194
	Every Day Is a New Day	195
	Have a Wish List	195
	The World Wants to Move Forward	196
	Can Management (and You!) Present a Convincing Business Case with Numbers in One Minute?	196
	Kitchen Sinking and Conservative Guidance	196
	The Market Is Lazy and Does Not Reward Complex Companies and Long-Term Developments	197
	Don't Be Too Eager Picking Up Stocks in a Downturn	197
	Watch Out for the Wallstreet Crowd!	197
	The Psychology of Numbers and Patterns	198
	Activism or Company Repositioning Takes Time	199
	Exploiting the Reversal Patterns for Similar Companies	199

Benefit from Benchmark Investors	200
Monitor Insider Trading and Shareholder Notifications	201

Acknowledgements	203
Appendix I: Some Terminology	207
Appendix II: Six Basic Valuation Metrics Explained	211
Appendix III: The Great Financial Crisis (GFC)	215
2004 – Cheap Credit	217
2005 – Securitisation	217
2006 – Strong Valuation Growth	218
2007 – Credit Crisis	219
2008 – Lehman Collapse	219
2009 – Balance Sheet Revival (Rights Issues)	220
2010 – Economic Uncertainty	221
2011 – Wait and See Attitude	222
2012 – Slow Recovery	223
About the Author	225
Index	227

Foreword

Real estate is the world's largest investment asset class. Yet, unlike stocks and bonds, broad-based, public ownership of real estate is a relatively recent phenomenon. Real estate investment trusts (REITs) were created in the US in 1960 to give individuals the opportunity to invest in diversified, income-producing real estate businesses. The 'Big Bang' moment for REITs came in 1986, when legislative changes in the US enabled REITs to actively manage and operate real estate, and not just own it passively. In 1993, new legislation also made it easier for pension funds to invest in real estate. The effect of these changes meant that, by 1994, the market capitalisation of US REITs had climbed to US$44 billion, from just US$9 billion in 1990.

It was around the same time – in the early 1990s – that investment firms, including the firm where I have spent the majority of my career, Blackstone (which today is the world's largest owner of commercial real estate), started programmatically investing in the sector. Firms such as ours responded to appetite from institutional investors for alternative and higher-yielding assets, thus helping to attract new sources of capital to the fledgling sector from pension funds, insurance companies, endowments, foundations and sovereign wealth funds.

This inflow of capital into the sector, coupled with increasingly professional management of real estate assets and companies, started to yield attractive returns for investors, which, in turn, helped build trust and confidence in the asset class. Continued positive investment outcomes encouraged investors to deploy increasing amounts of capital to real estate, in search of the sector's uncorrelated and out-sized returns at the time. This is exemplified across our business, e.g. by the growing size of many of our real estate funds, which are now in their tenth iteration and with our most recent global fund raising US$30 billion. Today, Blackstone's real estate business manages over US$336 billion of investor capital, with a portfolio valued at more than US$600 billion.

The rise of US REITs and private capital investment into real estate gave rise to public ownership of real estate. However, to ensure that the industry would continue to become a core part of institutional and individual investors' portfolios required more. For an industry which had relied primarily on relationships, increasing transparency and profession-alisation was required, including a focus on research, analysis, operational excellence and active asset management, as well as an understanding of capital markets and both cyclical and secular market trends.

Most importantly, the industry had to continue innovating. Occupier demand for real estate reflects the ways people live their lives: how and where they work, shop, sleep, travel and spend their disposable income. Successful real estate investors of the past 30 years have learned to pay attention to the demographic, societal and technological changes that impact occupier demand for real estate, and how that continuously evolves over time – changes that we see currently accelerating in fact, given rapid advances in technology.

Blackstone's approach and portfolio mix over time reflects this dynamic and thematic approach to investing. For example, the US office sector represented over 50% of our global equity portfolio in 2007, now it is less than 2%. Logistics, a sector that has benefited meaningfully from the e-commerce revolution, as well as – more recently – near-shoring trends, accounted for 2% of our portfolio in 2010. It now represents over 40%. Similarly, the explosive growth of content creation and storage, coupled with the rapid emergence of artificial intelligence (AI), are currently supporting data centres' ascendence to their new position as a mainstream real estate sector.

Foreword

Far from being static, the sector is always in flux and requires real estate investors to continuously challenge the status quo and seek new ways to marry conviction with opportunity.

When considering these requirements, no one is better placed than Harm Meijer to equip today's investors with the tools required to understand and navigate real estate markets. I have followed, respected and known Harm for essentially all of my career as a real estate investor. He was the most highly rated and most respected European real estate analyst for many years, and then co-founded ICAMAP, a leading European investment fund manager. These positions have given him a front row seat to observe the trends and cycles that have shaped real estate investing over the past two decades. Partly as a result, his ability to take complex subjects and translate them into relevant and meaningful insights for end investors is second to none.

This book is both important and timely. For the new generation of real estate investors, many of whom may have only experienced the post Global Financial Crisis (GFC)-investment cycle, the world of real estate over the past several years may have been unsettling. Harm's '20 Golden Rules of Real Estate' hold key lessons in this regard, from understanding the inherent cyclicality of real estate, and the opportunities that present themselves at the turn of each cycle, to the importance of prudent use of leverage and understanding the impact that interest rates can have on financing and capital markets.

Yet perhaps one of the book's most important contributions is Harm's analysis of the importance of value creation in real estate. This, we believe, is the key to performance in today's European real estate markets and to a degree helps explain why the European listed investment market has unfortunately historically lacked the scale and the depth of the US real estate market.

Despite a number of European countries launching their own REIT regimes over the past 20 years in the hope of replicating the success of US REITs, the success of each region's listed real estate companies have diverged significantly. While the US REIT market has gone from strength to strength, and today has a market capitalisation of over US$1.3 trillion, the European market remains a fraction of that.

Moreover, the listed European real estate market represents only 5% of the overall European commercial real estate market – in North America this proportion is significantly higher at 12%. In addition, the average equity market cap of listed commercial real estate companies in Europe is less than €1 billion, that is considerably smaller, and results in meaningfully reduced liquidity for investors, than from the average US REIT which is closer to US$5 billion.

A deeper pool of capital and a broad and engaged investor base has allowed US real estate markets to create sector champions, while the European listed universe, with some exceptions of course, remains more fragmented and has at times been more concentrated in country-focused generalists with mixed-sector portfolios. That has made it harder for investors to deploy capital with confidence, given the often divergent performance within subsectors of real estate.

While the US may have some inherent advantages, there are some non-structural disadvantages currently embedded in the structure of the European market, which Harm identifies and which can and should be addressed.

First, the focus on point-in-time performance metrics such as net asset value (NAV) in contrast to earnings and cash flow growth, which are more forward looking, can impair listed firms' ability to raise fresh capital to fund expansion or capitalise on investment opportunities. Second, an emphasis on dividends (versus total shareholder return) can create an inherent conflict between delivering short-term performance and delivering long-term value for shareholders. This deters those investors who believe companies should be focused on dynamic portfolio management for the benefit of long-term value creation. Both these phenomena have impacted companies' abilities to attract new sources of investor capital.

As large private market investors, we welcome any efforts to improve investor participation in public real estate markets. Any perceived dichotomy between public and private markets is illusory, as the relationship between the two is symbiotic. Private markets stand to benefit from a well-functioning public market, by providing both real-time price discovery as well as a viable avenue for exiting investments – through either mergers with existing listed companies or initial public offerings. Private markets, on the other hand, can offer public companies a way of accessing new sources of capital, allowing management teams to focus on value creation or implement meaningful changes across their businesses, rather than focusing on short-term performance or delivering a quarterly dividend. This can allow management teams to enact strategic initiatives away from the pressure of public markets.

Harm's work is an important step in bridging the gap between these seemingly contrasting approaches and broadening the investors' understanding of and access to the listed real estate markets. A deeper pool of capital, and a professionally managed sector, will create a flywheel effect, which will ultimately benefit public and private markets alike.

—James Seppala
Head of European Real Estate, Blackstone
London, September 2024

Preface

The real estate sector is a colourful world, seldom dull and often full of twists. While many perceive it as boring, safe and predictable, it is, in fact, a cyclical industry with frequent booms and busts. Investors can make substantial profits or lose everything. Moreover, the sector is filled with fascinating 'characters', making it an intriguing and entertaining asset class.

Recognising this from the outset 25 years ago, I began collecting boxes filled with materials, news articles, research notes, anecdotes, emails and diaries, all with the goal of writing a book – the very book that is now in front of you. As I have been fortunate to be active in this colourful sector in various roles, giving me a comprehensive 360-degree perspective, these boxes contained a wealth of information. A lot has happened over these years. The sector has emerged from the shadows and become more mature, but it has been quite a journey full of remarkable and turbulent times.

These boxes were stored at my mum's house all this time until she asked me two years ago what I was planning to do with them. It was time to start writing the book. A challenging period began with many early and late hours, and weekends in front of my laptop. Additionally, I conducted numerous interviews to verify the stories, add details or include the wisdom of key industry players, who are frequently quoted in this book.

Going through these boxes was an interesting exercise. Things were often slightly different from how I remembered them, and certain actions of mine seemed silly in hindsight (I guess I was still young...). Above all, the boxes contained captivating slogans, lessons and entertaining anecdotes. What was truly striking was that success stories in real estate consistently had the same ingredients, while failures repeatedly resulted from the same mistakes, time and time again.

Over the years, I have read numerous real estate books. However, most of them are focused on the US market: none clearly explained the golden rules for investing in European real estate companies or real estate investment trusts (REITs) from an industry insider's perspective, combined with real-life examples and anecdotes. That had to change. This is that book. Whilst the book is mainly focused on investing in listed property vehicles, the lessons drawn are also applicable for investing directly in real estate. After all, these companies hold real estate.

Doing your homework thoroughly, having great relationships, and acting on your convictions are some of the key takeaways in this book, but if I had to mention one key principle, it is 'trust'. Trust is the key to success. You break it once, it is hard to restore, although you might be lucky with hard work over time. But you break it twice, it is gone. Gone forever. You are in the black box.

This is true for people you interact with, work with and deal with. It also applies to the equity market. Once trust is gone, companies find themselves in a very delicate sliding situation, which we will discuss further in this book and call the 'vicious downward spiral of doom', which is difficult to break, let alone reverse. Things can go very fast in this spiral, and one should expect the unexpected. The equity market does not like uncertainty and definitely not lost trust. There is this saying: 'If in doubt, throw it out'. Meaning: if you doubt the intentions of a company or what is the truth, just sell the shares!

I do hope you enjoy reading this book, that sometimes it will make you smile or even amaze you. But above all, that it makes you think and makes you a better and more successful investor.

Introduction – A Sector Not To Be Ignored

Real Estate Is an Important Asset Class

$380 Trillion Market

Real estate is an important investment class as it provides for both living and economic activity. Besides, it is the largest investment class globally, surpassing publicly traded equities and debt securities, with values of $380 trillion, $99 trillion and $130 trillion, respectively. According to Savills (Figure I.1), residential real estate accounts for the majority of this global value at $288 trillion (76%), followed by commercial real estate at $51 trillion (13%) and agricultural land at $41 trillion (11%). Based on the global GDP in 2022 of $101 trillion, this total value equates to 3.8× GDP.

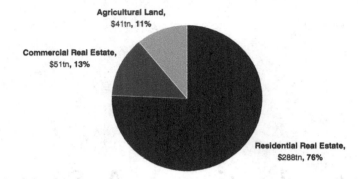

Figure I.1 Total value of global real estate in 2022
Source: Adapted from Savills (2023) 'Global real estate universe in comparison, 2022'. https://www.savills.com/impacts/market-trends/the-total-value-of-global-real-estate-property-remains-the-worlds-biggest-store-of-wealth.html.

Europe makes up about 20–25% of the global real estate market, with the largest markets being Germany ($17 trillion, 4% of global), the UK ($12 trillion, 3%) and France ($11 trillion, 3%).

Wide Range of Investors

Approximately 26% of European commercial property is held as an investment (see Figure I.2), while 74% is in the hands of owner-occupiers. The largest investors are non-listed funds, holding 35% of the market, followed by other professional investors, such as high net worth individuals and alternative investment managers, with 30%, and listed property companies with 19%. Listed companies are real estate vehicles that are publicly traded on a stock exchange. Most of them have the real estate investment trust (REIT) status, which generally means they pay no tax on rental profit and capital gains but must distribute the majority of their recurring earnings as dividends, on which tax is due. Institutional investors account for approximately 8% of the investment in European real estate, though they also hold significant amounts in non-listed and listed vehicles. This is similar for non-EU institutions and sovereign wealth funds, estimated at 7%, but in reality, their share, including their stakes in vehicles, is much higher. Indeed, global investment has increasingly become an important source of capital in the European real estate market.

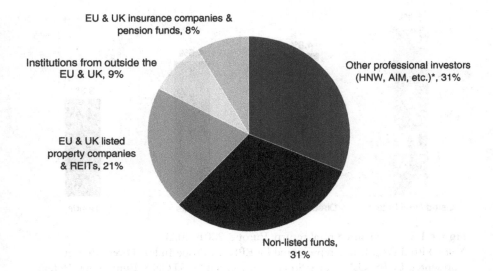

Figure I.2 Commercial real estate holdings by investor type in 2023 – EU and UK
*HNW – high net worth individuals; AIM – Alternative Investment Managers.

Source: RHL Strategic Solutions estimates using data from Eurostat, ECB, EPRA, INREV, OECD, ONS and MSCI, 2023.

Attractive Long-Term Returns

Investors in property benefit from rental income and changes in the building's value over time. The sector has provided superior returns. For example, over the period from 2001 to 2023 (the longest period for which INREV[1] direct fund data are available), listed real estate companies performed best with an annual return of 5.8%, followed by direct real estate funds with 4.8%, equities with 4.6% and bonds with 3.3% (Figure I.3).

In the long term, real estate stocks, i.e. listed property companies, have delivered between 9% and 10% per annum, which is an excellent return for the asset class compared to alternatives. For instance, a real estate index for listed UK property stocks has generated an annualised return of 9.7% since 1965. Its 50-year moving average has been between 8% and 12% (Figure I.4).

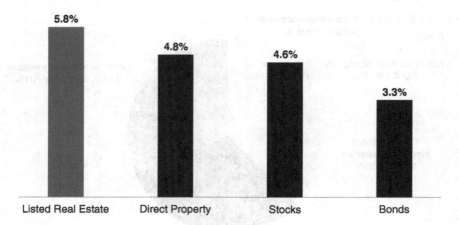

Figure I.3 Annualised total return, Europe, 2001–2023
Notes: Listed Real Estate represented by EPRA Europe Index; Direct Property represented by INREV Index; Stocks represented by STOXX Europe 600 Index; Bonds represented by the Bloomberg Europe Aggregate Index.

Source: Data from Factset, except for INREV data: https://www.inrev.org/market-information/indices/inrev-index#Latestpublications.

Real Estate Enhances the Risk/Return Profile of Investment Portfolios

There is no debate: the addition of real estate improves the risk/reward profile of investment portfolios compared to equities, bonds and other

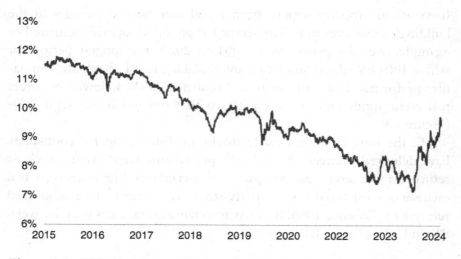

Figure I.4 UK Listed Property Index, annual total return – 50-year rolling
Source: Author's estimates based on historical stock statistics and EPRA.

Introduction – A Sector Not To Be Ignored

alternative investments. However, there is more discussion about the exact allocation. Whilst research continuously shows that the optimal portion of real estate in an investment portfolio is between circa 9% (e.g. Kallberg and Liu, 1996)[2] and 15–20% (e.g. Amédée-Manesme et al., 2019),[3] in reality the allocation of institutional investors tends to be on the low side of this range at around 7–10%. For example, McKinsey found target allocations for institutional investors ranged 9–10% between 2011 and 2015.[4] Based on my experience and the cyclical nature of the asset class, I believe an average allocation of circa 15% is ideal with a range of 10–20% depending on the stage of the cycle. Given real estate's illiquid and rather opaque features (see next section), I recommend allocating circa half of the real estate portion to listed real estate companies or REITs.

Two Undesirable Features of Real Estate

However, there are two undesirable features of investing in real estate: it is illiquid and opaque.

Illiquid

The biggest issue is that real estate itself is an illiquid investment. It takes time to buy or sell a property. Potential buyer pools can be significantly smaller for larger assets or during downturns when liquidity can dry up completely. Additionally, there is a risk of buying an asset that turns out to be a poor investment, e.g. due to changing tenant demand, in which case repositioning the property could be extremely costly. As Evert Jan van Garderen, CEO of Eurocommercial Properties, said to me: 'It is not difficult to buy a property, but to sell it is'.

Opaque

Although sector transparency has increased over the years, real estate is an opaque asset class, e.g. in terms of pricing, valuation, ownership and actors in the space. Real estate markets frequently depend greatly on local knowledge and insider information.

Gladly, there are ways to invest in the space with increased liquidity and transparency.

Listed Real Estate Has Attractive Features

There are different ways to invest in real estate: directly, through a fund structure or via other methods such as a club-deal or joint venture, but we will focus on the first two. The most common types of funds are closed-ended non-listed, closed-ended listed and open-ended non-listed funds.

Non-listed closed-ended funds are not listed on a stock exchange and have a fixed maturity date, typically around 10 years. Although participations can sometimes be traded on the secondary market, this is usually at a significant valuation discount. Listed closed-ended funds or REITs are traded on a stock exchange and have a perpetual structure, meaning the fund has no set end date. Non-listed open-ended funds are not listed on a stock exchange and aim to provide liquidity to investors by maintaining a cash reserve or disposing of assets for redemptions.

Table I.1 displays my assessment of investing in real estate directly or via one of these fund structures. Every structure has its pros and cons, but in my view, listed real estate has the most attractive characteristics, although it is not perfect. Careful analysis of assets, the balance sheet and management is essential for every investment vehicle.

Table I.1 Investor considerations (score 1 to 3 with 3 being best)

	Direct	Closed-ended (non-listed)	Closed-ended (listed)	Open-ended
Portfolio diversification	1	2	3	2
Liquidity	2	1	3	1.5
Return volatility	3	3	1	2
ESG	1	2	3	2
Financing	1	2	3	2
Management intensity	1	3	3	3
Alignment management – investor	3	2	1	1
Costs	1	1	3	1
Tax	1	3	3	3
Total	14	19	23	17.5

Source: Author.

Listed real estate scores well on several fronts:

Portfolio diversification: With thousands of listed property companies worldwide investing in various sectors, investors can build a truly diversified portfolio. This type of diversification is not possible through investing in funds, let alone directly by yourself. Worse still, I have seen numerous private investors making large bets on individual assets, which turned out to be disastrous.

Liquidity: Listed property stocks can be bought or sold with a mouse click. However, it takes time to sell or buy a property, while investors in non-listed closed-ended funds are locked in for a certain period. Whilst open-ended funds promise liquidity, this is frequently false, particularly in downturns when investors want to withdraw their capital but assets cannot be sold, causing these funds to 'close their gates'. As a result, listed stocks have instant pricing, whereas the other options depend on valuations that typically lag behind market reality.

ESG: Listed companies are frequently leaders in ESG (environmental, social and governance) initiatives, as their actions are subject to public scrutiny.

Financing: Listed vehicles typically have wider access to financing, such as from banks, private placements and public bond markets.

Management intensity: Property investments require intense management. The three fund structures handle the management on behalf of the investor.

Costs: Management costs are often relatively high for non-listed funds, particularly those targeting private individuals. Listed real estate companies can usually generate platform value, a benefit that is more difficult for smaller funds and, especially, for individual investors to achieve. For example, the average management cost as a percentage of the portfolio value for listed REIT Unibail-Rodamco-Westfield (URW) is 0.45% per annum, while the cost for an individual in a non-listed fund can be as high as 2–3% and in some cases even much higher.

Tax: Funds generally have tax-efficient structures available. For example, many listed companies have the option to become a REIT. This option is sometimes available for non-listed funds as well, or they can benefit from other tax-efficient schemes. A clear advantage of investing in a listed property company is that the company has already paid for transfer duties (the tax payable when a property is purchased, which can be as high as 5–10%, depending on the jurisdiction), whereas this still has to be paid if one invests directly in real estate or in a fund that has yet to buy the assets.

Whilst one can debate my assessment and call me biased, listed property does tackle the two main drawbacks of investing in real estate: the liquidity issue and the sector being opaque. In particular, the arrival of

REITs in Europe has improved disclosure and provided better insight into the wheeling and dealing in the underlying property markets. Besides, it has made property more accessible for investors and provided liquidity to an otherwise illiquid asset class.

But Listed Real Estate Is Not Always Preferred (Although It Should Be!)

However, many investors still prefer direct investment or non-listed funds over listed real estate, primarily for two reasons.

Alignment Between Investor and Manager

The best alignment between the investor and manager is, of course, when the investor manages the property themselves, i.e. directly. Additionally, closed-ended fund structures often have better management incentives than perpetual ones, as the manager knows the real estate will have to be disposed of one day. This is a positive aspect, as it is factored into their investment process from the beginning: who will be the next buyer? Listed companies should adopt the same thinking. For them, it is immensely important to scrutinise the management incentive packages. Too often, there have been listed management teams who enriched themselves but not the investor. Although this has improved over time, it still deserves proper analysis and is a topic we will cover in detail in this book.

Volatility

Secondly, listed real estate is often perceived as too volatile in the short term because of its continuous pricing. Investors do not like volatility; they want a steady rising return. They believe, much to the frustration of the listed real estate world, that non-listed real estate provides this. But this is incorrect. It is a strange phenomenon where the whole industry, including investors, banks, insurance companies and accountants, bury their heads in the sand and pretend that non-listed property is significantly less volatile than publicly traded real estate. In fact, in 2024, the supervision newsletter 'Commercial real estate valuations: insights from on-site inspections' by the European Central Bank (ECB) concluded that banks and their valuers frequently overlook changing market conditions when valuing commercial real estate portfolios. Instances were identified where appraisals were based on 2021 transaction data, as 'there was no evidence that the market value had fallen' – despite clear declines in 2022–2023.

Listed Real Estate Pricing Is Closer to Reality

It is true that the pricing of listed real estate can be impacted by daily 'noise', but its valuation is often much closer to reality than non-listed property valuations. According to the study 'Asset allocations, returns, volatilities, Sharpe Ratios, and investment costs experienced by large European institutional investors, 2005–2021' by CEM Benchmarking in September 2023, the correlation between listed and non-listed real estate was much higher – 86% versus 27% reported – once the valuation data was adjusted for smoothing, lagging and leverage. In fact, the issue is that valuations do not properly take liquidity into account.

Liquidity Equals Value

In addition, as Sam Zell, the famous father of US REITs, used to say 'liquidity equals value!'[5] While investors in non-listed real estate often get stuck – e.g. when the transaction market is closed in a downturn, when an investment fails or when a fund still has a significant number of years to run – listed real estate can be sold instantly. Many investors do not understand the true value of this. Listed real estate offers liquidity at all times, giving investors the opportunity to convert holdings into cash and re-invest subsequently.

Listed Real Estate Is a Great Hunting Ground and Poised for Growth

Not only does publicly traded real estate have attractive features, but the European market is also a great hunting ground for investors. There are approximately 400 listed property companies in Europe with a total market capitalisation of around €470 billion (as of July 2024). These companies have diverse country and sector allocations: about 27% invest in multiple sectors, 25% in logistics, 21% in residential, 12% in retail and 8% in offices (Figure I.5).

As most fund managers focus on a benchmark index, many companies are not on their radar. For instance, the EPRA Europe benchmark index contains approximately 103 stocks, with the top 40 accounting for about 80% of the index. This means that more or less 60 stocks in the index have a modest weighting, whereas 300 are not in the index at all. These 360 stocks receive little attention from analysts and investors. It is no coincidence that well-known private equity players, such as Blackstone, Brookfield and TPG, have been acquiring undervalued listed companies in recent years.

However, I believe that the European listed real estate market will experience strong growth in the coming years due to rebounding property valuations, its attractive features, well-positioned companies (in terms of quality assets and balance sheets) and management's willingness to expand by acquiring assets and raising equity.

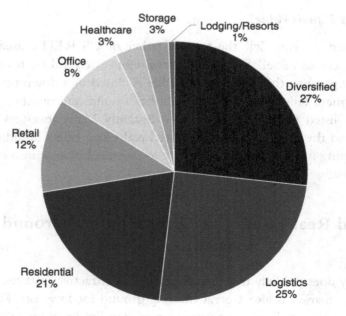

Figure I.5 Sector split, EPRA Europe
Source: Adapted from EPRA, May 2024.

Introduction – A Sector Not To Be Ignored

Denominator Effect

The denominator effect works as follows: Several investors, such as pension funds, work with target investment allocations: X% in real estate, X% in equities, X% in bonds, etc. If prices in certain categories suddenly fall, as was the case with equities and bonds in 2022, the weighting of other investment classes, such as real estate, shoots up. As a result, pension funds end up with a disproportionately high allocation to the outperforming segments and, consequently, will limit their future allocations to these investments or start to reduce/sell them.

It is a peculiar process, because in reality, real estate valuations lag the market, and therefore this overweight in real estate does not exist to the extent that these investors believe, as actual pricing is lower than real estate appraisals indicate. There is simply a lack of transaction evidence. This investment process bears the risk of being too late to act and being behind the curve, which can lead to an overshooting market. It is important to understand this phenomenon because this rebalancing of portfolios is a slow process and can 'hang over' the market for some time, prolonging downturns or resulting in an overshooting market.

Book Organisation

In this book, we discuss 20 golden rules for investing in real estate, split across four parts: I. Real Estate, II. Capital Structure, III. Management and IV. Investing in Listed Real Estate.

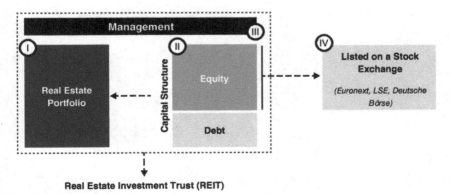

The book is written from the perspective of listed real estate investment companies, as these offer the highest level of transparency, real-time pricing and liquidity, providing a better understanding of the intricacies of the property market. However, the key takeaways are applicable to other types of real estate investors, such as individuals purchasing real estate themselves or investing in real estate funds not listed on a stock exchange.

Notes

1. INREV is the European Association for Investors in Non-Listed Real Estate.
2. J.G. Kallberg and C.H. Liu (1996) 'The role of real estate in the portfolio allocation process', *Real Estate Economics* 24(3). https://papers.ssrn.com/sol3/papers.cfm?abstract_id=9140
3. C.-O. Amédée-Manesme, F. Barthélémy, P. Bertrand and J.-L. Prigent (2019) 'Mixed-asset portfolio allocation under mean-reverting asset returns', *Annals of Operations Research* 281: 65–98. https://doi.org/10.1007/s10479-018-2761-y
4. McKinsey (2017) 'Understanding real estate as an investment class'. https://www.mckinsey.com/industries/real-estate/our-insights/understanding-real-estate-as-an-investment-class#/
5. Sam Zell (2017) *Am I being too subtle?* (New York: Random House), p. 104.

The 20 Golden Rules of Real Estate

Real Estate

1. High yield for a reason
2. Look for a rent compounding machine with minimum capex
3. Scan for value-add potential
4. Real estate is cyclical
5. Expected returns should beat cost of capital
6. Central bank and government stimuli (or lack of it) can be game changers

Capital Structure

7. Prudent use of financial leverage: don't get caught out by downturns
8. Don't assume that financing will always be available

Management

9. Continuous value creation is key
10. Radical action needed in case of shareholder value destruction
11. Overconfidence leads to downfall
12. Corporate governance should be top nudge

Investing in Listed Real Estate

13. Scrutinise property investment vehicles
14. Significant upside based on multicriteria valuations
15. Focus on (upcoming) value creators, be careful with destroyers
16. Look for maximum pessimism and maximum optimism
17. Ensure management, the board and other stakeholders are aligned with investment objectives
18. Be aware of self-liquidating companies
19. When trust is gone, there is no limit to downside
20. Understand the stock market (rules)

Part I

Real Estate

The target should be to invest in a yielding cash flow machine, which is generating compounded rental growth with value-add potential, that significantly beats the cost of capital, at the right time in the cycle.

Chapter 1

High Yield for a Reason

It is the classic mistake: buying real estate solely because the yield – rent as a percentage of the property value – is high. Of course, one can get lucky, for instance with a distressed seller, but more often it is a sign of a 'dressed-up' asset with poor rental income prospects. As Michiel te Paske, former fund manager of Morgan Stanley, says: 'You can't polish a turd'. But it is remarkable how many investors fall into this trap time and again. Particularly, private investors and smaller pension funds have been victims of buying assets for the yield, only to end up with declining rental income and almost worthless vacant buildings. The property might offer a high yield, but it is about the total return (yield plus valuation growth). In my experience, the high yield is often not high enough to compensate for the risk. In fact, there is often an inverse relationship between yield and total return: lower-yielding assets generating a high future total return and high-yielding real estate producing a low total return. So, if a property or real estate investment product offers an attractive yield, it is essential to dig deeper. What needs to be properly checked: how is the yield exactly calculated and is it a good asset?

17

How Is the Yield Exactly Calculated?
Is It 'Dressed Up'?

Companies often state that they purchased a property or portfolio at a yield of x%. The yield is calculated by dividing the rent by the value of the property, but the question is, what is included in rent and value? Frequently, the yield is presented more favourably than the investor believes it to be. Therefore, a careful check of the definition is important, such as what rent is used and which costs are taken into account.

For example, regarding the numerator ('rent'), does it include gross rent (rent received) or net rent (after operating costs), cash or accountancy income, any (future) reversionary potential and certain costs? Regarding the denominator ('value'), does it incorporate purchaser's costs? These are costs such as taxes and agency fees that the buyer must pay for purchasing the property. Depending on the answers, the yield can be significantly different. For example, in Table 1.1, the range can be as wide as 5.6–8%!

Table 1.1 Yield calculation

	Scenario 1 Gross reversionary yield	Scenario 2 Gross yield	Scenario 3 Net yield excl. purchasers' costs	Scenario 4 Net yield incl. purchasers' costs
Rent	8 (Reversionary)	7 (Gross)	6 (Net)	6 (Net)
Value	100 (Net)	100 (Net)	100 (Net)	108 (Gross)
Yield	**8.0%**	**7.0%**	**6.0%**	**5.6%**

Source: Author.

In the first scenario, the yield is estimated in the most favourable way: a gross reversionary rent of 8% – the rent the tenant currently pays plus any expected future uplifts from filling vacancies, positive rent reviews or contractual uplifts – divided by the agreed purchase price. In scenario 2, the gross yield is shown (the rent paid divided by the agreed purchase price). Scenarios 3 and 4 are both based on the net rent (the rent paid by the tenant minus operating costs), but the first is divided by the agreed purchase price, while the latter includes purchasers' costs in the agreed price (called the gross value).

I could have added more possible yield calculations. For instance, UK companies publish an equivalent yield, which is a time-weighted average of the net initial yield and the reversionary yield, representing the return a property will produce based on the timing of the income to be received. Additionally, I could have made the examples more detailed, as any item can be broken down repeatedly, e.g. which costs are exactly taken into account in the operating costs?

The actual European Public Real Estate Association (EPRA) recommendation to calculate the EPRA net yield is to take the annualised rental income based on the cash rents passing at the balance sheet date, less non-recoverable property operating expenses, divided by the gross market value of the property. It is closest to scenario 4 in Table 1.1, i.e. the least favourable interpretation. I prefer this definition as it is cash based and takes all relevant costs into account. There is also an EPRA topped-up net initial yield, which adds back rent-free periods and guaranteed upcoming rental uplifts. Of course, companies can, and I believe should, add an adjusted EPRA net yield calculation if they believe the recommended calculation excludes certain items that are important for their business.

Is It a Good Asset?

This is unfortunately often not the case. It has a high yield because the rental growth outlook is weak or negative, or there is a high risk of the asset becoming vacant. For example, the property might be located in the middle of nowhere, be threatened by future supply of new buildings, have a short-term lease with a rent significantly above the market level, have a shaky tenant and/or no longer meet occupier requirements. In addition, vacancy costs and capital expenditure to keep the property attractive for tenants will only increase. A negative spiral begins, repeatedly ending in a completely vacant building where alternative use, such as transforming an office into residential property, becomes the only option. However, this is frequently only lucrative after a significant write-down. There have been countless cases like this, which went from bad to worse.

For example, in the first decade of the 21st century, there was a Dutch office company with the slogan 'Dividend Is King'. Many retail investors bought into it and were literally celebrating the dividend at each annual general meeting (AGM). However, to achieve the high dividend yield, it invested in offices in weak locations with rent guarantees given by the developers. When the office market turned, the offices became vacant, and the developers could not fulfil their obligations. The empire fell apart.

Another well-known example is when UK property companies British Land and Landsec sold the 460,000 sq. ft. Bon Accord and St Nicholas shopping centres, plus some adjoining properties in Aberdeen, for £189 million, reportedly at a 6.65% net yield (net rental income divided by valuation including purchasers' costs) in October 2013. It seemed like a nice yield when monetary conditions were loose: at the time, the Bank of England (BoE) rate was only 0.5%, and the five-year swap rate was 1.3%. However, the mall entered a negative spiral, being hit by e-commerce, competition and COVID-19. It was sold again for below £10 million (rumoured price £8 million) in 2023. The irony was that the once 'high' yield only rose higher and higher over time as income growth prospects deteriorated and the value declined.

Note that property can sometimes go down to zero or even negative value, e.g. because there is no expectation of future income, high outgoing costs (e.g. utilities, maintenance and taxes) and high capital expenditure to reposition the asset. During the Global Financial Crisis (GFC) in 2007–2009 (discussed in more detail in Appendix III), there were cases in Spain where land prices were effectively negative, considering all relevant factors.

Chapter 2

Look for a Rent Compounding Machine with Minimum Capex

The concept of compounding is followed by many successful CEOs, as it generates strong returns over time, often more than one would initially expect. For example, if one achieves a 10% annual return for eight consecutive years, the capital invested would double. Similarly, if one starts investing early in life, a 6% annual return would result in 3.2 times the original amount after 20 years. Andrew Jones, CEO London-Metric, says: 'We believe that income compounding is the eight Wonder of the World - the secret ingredient that creates wealth over time.'

To create a compounding machine, it is essential to compound rental income (i.e. grow income steadily over time), as this ultimately leads to compounding capital growth. Compounding can be further enhanced by reinvesting proceeds back into the business instead of returning them to investors.

Compound Interest											
	2%	4%	5%	6%	8%	10%	15%	20%	25%	30%	40%
2 years	1.0	1.1	1.1	1.1	1.2	1.2	1.3	1.4	1.6	1.7	2.0
3 years	1.1	1.1	1.2	1.2	1.3	1.3	1.5	1.7	2.0	2.2	2.7
4 years	1.1	1.2	1.2	1.3	1.4	1.5	1.7	2.1	2.4	2.9	3.8
5 years	1.1	1.2	1.3	1.3	1.5	1.6	2.0	2.5	3.1	3.7	5.4
8 years	1.2	1.3	1.4	1.5	1.8	2.0	2.9	3.9	5.3	7.2	12.5
10 years	1.2	1.5	1.6	1.8	2.2	2.6	4.0	6.2	9.3	13.8	28.9
15 years	1.3	1.8	2.1	2.4	3.2	4.2	8.1	15.4	28.4	51.2	155.6
20 years	1.5	2.2	2.7	3.2	4.7	6.7	16.4	38.3	86.7	190.0	836.7
25 years	1.6	2.7	3.4	4.3	6.8	10.8	32.9	95.4	264.7	705.6	4,499.9
30 years	1.8	3.2	4.3	5.7	10.1	17.4	66.2	237.4	807.8	2,620.0	24,201.4

www.londonmetric.com
LondonMetric Property Plc
One Curzon St, London W1J 5HB

Source: Back of business card – Andrew Jones, CEO, LondonMetric.

A strong rent compounding machine has the following characteristics: real estate with strong supply/demand dynamics coupled with the ability to capture rental growth with minimum capital expenditure (capex) and minimum tenant incentives.

Real Estate with Strong Supply/Demand Dynamics

The scarcer the asset, the higher the rental growth potential. It is key to identify the winning real estate sectors, i.e. the sectors with the best supply and demand fundamentals in the future. These sectors will have the best rental growth prospects. One wants to be a price setter, not a price taker.

Supply

How is the property positioned (in terms of location and offering) versus competing buildings now and in the future? How easy is it for others to build a competing product? A simple look at Google Maps and future supply assessments from property agents is a good start to the analysis. As we will see also later, the concept of replacement value is important, i.e. if the

Look for a Rent Compounding Machine with Minimum Capex   23

replacement value (the cost of land plus construction costs) is high versus today's building valuations, developers are unlikely to start new projects, but if it is low, new competing projects are likely to be started in due course.

The following example from the Amsterdam office market is illustrative. Amsterdam was suffering from a persistently high office vacancy after the burst of the dot-com bubble, with vacancy rates ranging between 15% and 20%. Some areas had even higher vacancy, whilst new offices were still being built. The issue was that each city in the Netherlands competed with a neighbouring municipality for companies, as it would bring money for the local government (from the sale of land) and jobs for the community. Developers were happy to build, and companies were happy to play local governments off against each other to get the lowest land price. Frequently, investors, typically a pension fund, were on the receiving end, as businesses kept moving, leaving them with outdated vacant offices, which subsequently plummeted in value. There were numerous examples of tragic situations, with the most famous one being where KPMG moved to a neighbouring property, leaving a vacant office behind in Amstelveen, which was now worth 50% less on my estimates. It was only when planning became stricter, and offices were converted into residential, that vacancy rates started to fall and the market became healthier. From 2013 onwards, vacancy gradually started to decline to a low of circa 5% by the first half of 2022.

Some types of property will always be in demand and cannot be replicated. Anybody can assemble a portfolio of random shops tomorrow, but it is impossible to buy significant exposure in well-known historic locations, such as Chinatown and Covent Garden in London. The key question is: how hard is it to replicate this portfolio? The harder, the better. Sure, these assets will also go up and down in price, but they will provide superior returns over time: 'Hold fast that which is good'.

For example, the performance of London West End offices has historically been much stronger than city offices, because the former market is more supply-constrained (Figure 2.1). I would be more cautious about investing in properties that are easier to replicate and see them more as trading assets. This is typically true for offices, which can face increased competition over time. As an executive said: 'When the last tenant moved in, the building should be sold'. As a result, supply-constrained properties tend to be strong inflation hedges over time, whilst this is not the case for assets located in areas with unlimited building potential.

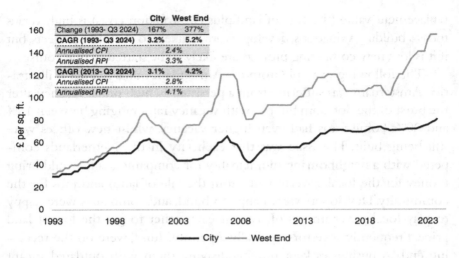

Figure 2.1 City and West End – prime office rents
Source: CBRE 2024.

Location plays a big role in future supply, but it is also about the product offered to tenants, e.g. what is the carbon intensity of a building (kg CO_2 per sq. m), size of floor plates, type of rental contract and amenities in the nearby area or in the property.

There Is Too Much Retail Space!

Dutch retail property company Corio entered Germany by buying a shopping centre portfolio for €1.3 billion in March 2010. Later, it hosted a property trip for investors and analysts to visit the malls, starting in Berlin. As part of these investor days, the management of Corio gave a presentation and had also paid for an independent research house, bulwiengesa, to present their views on the German retail property market. It would be a remarkable event. Bulwiengesa's view was truly independent, but not positive! This research house not only showed a long-term series of declining sales per square metre for the German retail market – a leading indicator for future rental growth – its presenter was also not amused, to say the least, about Corio developing another centre in Berlin: 'There is too much retail space in Berlin, too much!' He was almost shouting this. Almost angry. Multiple times. Whilst he was presenting, management was cringing in the front row. Oh dear! During the trip, we saw the CEO staring from a balustrade into one of the malls we were visiting, and we wondered: 'Does he regret the deal?' The presenter would be proven right in the years to come.

Interestingly, I had a similar experience a bit later, but this time in Tallinn, Estonia. We chose not to invest in a company because there was already an excess of shopping mall space, and this particular company was building another one next to Tallinn's best mall. Indeed, the lettings were underwhelming, and the mall eventually went into administration. However, what the company did well was that the project was largely financed by a European lender with a secured loan. Consequently, the lender suffered significant losses.

Demand

To assess future demand, it is crucial to have a view on:

- **The macro-economic outlook for the area**, e.g. economic growth, retail sales, income growth and job creation.
- **Tenant requirements**, one needs to deeply understand the tenants, e.g. what kind of space and amenities are they looking for? What (digital) infrastructure do they need? What trends are occupiers seeing? What is their vision of the future?
- **Structural trends**, e.g. those driven by demographics, technology (such as artificial intelligence blockchain, 3D printing, virtual and augmented reality, nanotechnology, and biotechnology) and climate change. These trends can affect tenant demand, for instance, by increasing the need for elderly homes, online shopping, working from home (WFH) and sustainable buildings.
- **Future competitiveness of the area**, e.g. are there any significant infrastructure projects planned? For example, academic research shows that the opening of a new trainline within 800 metre of a property will increase its attractiveness and adds between 5% and 10% to the value of the building.

Crossrail

In 2011, we (the JP Morgan Property Research team) published a detailed study on the potential impact of the new Crossrail train line (later renamed the Elizabeth line). This new high-frequency, high-capacity rail link was approved in 2007, with construction beginning in 2009. It would run from the western suburbs of London, including Heathrow Airport, through the heart of the city (Bond Street and Tottenham Court Road) to the eastern suburbs, including the business district Canary Wharf. We mapped all the properties of the listed landlords to assess which landlord would benefit the most. The study was a great success. The only issue: Crossrail was expected to open in 2018, but it was heavily delayed due to COVID and archaeological findings. The first part opened in May 2022, and it was fully operational a year later...

Direct Market Studies/Models

Too often, analysts and investors do not carry out their own supply/demand studies but instead rely on the opinion of conflicted parties such as companies themselves, agents or the financial community. It is good to listen to them, but investors should also make their own analysis and models to understand the drivers of a certain market, how these variables interact and what the outlook for key parameters, such as vacancy, is in the coming years. Frequently, one would arrive at a more nuanced outlook and, for sure, spot turning points before others do.

It is really fascinating how much data is publicly available to make a detailed market study. Let's look at two examples: the office model and dominance analysis for shopping centres.

Office Model. The office model is my favourite because it really made a difference for me in spotting changing trends at an early stage, especially as numerous market commentators stay too positive or too negative for too long – or are always positive! The office model forecasts future vacancy, as it is the driver for rental growth. Demand for office space is a function of future office job growth and the required space per square

Look for a Rent Compounding Machine with Minimum Capex 27

metre per person, whilst supply is estimated by the new buildings being delivered to the market and old ones being demolished. Note that it takes time to construct a building, which means that the expected deliveries in the coming two years are unlikely to change.

It is key to find consistent data that can be combined and to play around with the input, especially future job growth, to see the impact on vacancy under different scenarios. Simply said, a vacancy rate below 5–7% means rents are growing, whereas rents are falling above these vacancy levels. There are always exceptions, as there might be strong/weak demand for a certain type of building or floor size within the office market, but that is the rule of thumb. Table 2.1 shows an example of the office model I made in 2009, predicting that London city office vacancy levels would fall in the near future after the hit of the Global Financial Crisis and that subsequently rents would start to grow again. This did happen, although vacancy reduced slower than expected, but rents started to bottom out and increase, underpinning our investment case.

Table 2.1 London city office model

	2H2009E	**2010E**	**2011E**	**2012E**
Stock start (000s sq. ft.)	91,030	91,056	90,549	89,083
Vacant space start (000s sq. ft.)	13,290	14,227	11,467	7,229
Vacancy start (%)	**14.6%**	**15.6%**	**12.7%**	**8.1%**
Employment growth (%)	1.0%	2.5%	3.0%	3.0%
Employment (000s)	782	802	826	851
Net demand office space (000s sq. ft.)	910	2,253	2,771	2,854
New supply (000s sq. ft.)	1,392	2,225	1,250	3,000
Demolition stock (000s sq. ft.)	1,365	2,732	2,716	2,672
Stock end (000s sq. ft.)	91,056	90,549	89,083	89,410
Vacant space end (000s sq. ft.)	14,227	11,467	7,229	4,703
Vacancy end (%)	**15.6%**	**12.7%**	**8.1%**	**5.3%**

Source: BNP Real Estate, CBRE, Savills (for actual data).

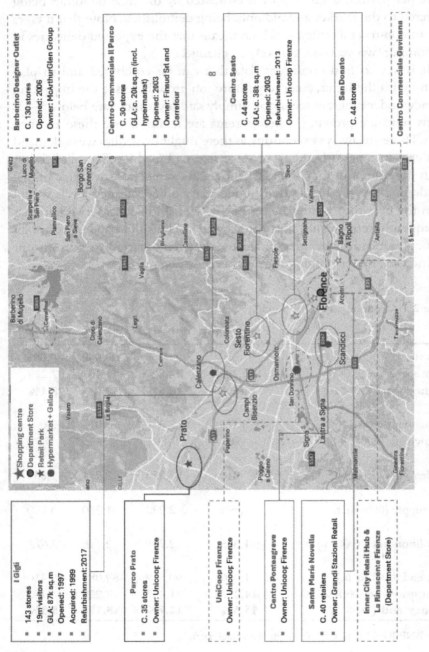

Figure 2.2 Eurocommercial Properties: I Gigli, Florence – the largest shopping centre in Tuscany
Source: Companies, Google, shopping centre websites.

Look for a Rent Compounding Machine with Minimum Capex 29

Dominance Analysis. Another useful analysis is to assess whether a shopping mall is dominant in its catchment area by evaluating whether it has the leading brands. This can be done simply by counting which mall has most of the key leading retailers. For example, the shopping centre I Gigli in Florence, owned by real estate company Eurocommercial Properties, had by far the best line-up compared to the alternative destinations for shoppers (see Figure 2.2). It is the place to be for retailers and consumers. This analysis is particularly important in times of excess retail space and the threat from the Internet.

The dominance analysis in Figure 2.3 indicates that I Gigli hosts most of Italy's top brands, making it the most dominant shopping mall in the region.

Centre	I Gigli, Florence	Il Parco	Parco Prato	Centro Sesto	San Donato	Barberino Designer Outlet	Centro Ponteagreve	Santa Maria Novella – Grandi Stazioni
Driving time		10 min	14 min	16 min	16 min	22 min	22 min	35 min
Rank	#1	#7	#4	#3	#6	#2	#7	#4
# Stores (c.)	143	30	35	44	44	130	25	40
Nike	✓					✓		
Apple Store	✓							
Primark	✓							
Adidas	✓					✓		
Clarks	✓					✓		
Puma	✓					✓		
Douglas	✓							
Zara	✓							
Pandora	✓							
Swarovski	✓							
H&M	✓		✓		✓			
Lush	✓							
Lacoste	✓					✓		
McDonald's	✓					✓		✓
Timberland	✓					✓		
Coop	✓		✓	✓	✓	✓	✓	
Bata	✓			✓				
Levi's	✓					✓		
Guess	✓							
Calvin Klein	✓					✓		
Carrefour		✓						
Total Top Brands	45	5	8	11	7	25	5	8
As % of retailers	31%	17%	23%	25%	16%	19%	20%	20%

Figure 2.3 I Gigli dominance analysis
Source: ICAMAP Advisory.

Ability to Capture Rental Growth Potential

After identifying the type of real estate that has the best rental growth prospects, the next question is how this rental growth potential can be captured (or how defensively it is positioned in the event of a downturn). Simply put, if rental prospects are great, a landlord prefers short-term leases to capture this growth immediately when it arrives. If prospects are dim, he/she prefers long-term contracts.

The following points are important to assess.

30 REAL ESTATE RULES

Quality of the Asset

Its (micro) location: Is the property in the right location or is it, e.g. outside the shopper flow or not close to transport links?

The quality/standards/layout of the building: Is this the type of property tenants are looking for?

Leasing Strategy

Price versus occupancy: How will the rent be maximised over time? How is the building positioned in the market? What kind of tenants are targeted? How does management approach the leasing process? To quote Evert Jan van Garderen: 'Leasing excellence is not about leasing the first unit but leasing the last unit'.

Type of Rental Contract

Contractual uplifts: Is the annual rent indexation linked to a Consumer Price Index (CPI; typical on the continent of Europe) or a fixed percentage? Is there a five-year upward-only rent review, as is most common in the UK?

Tenant churn: Is it easy to remove or change a tenant? The easier it is to rotate occupiers, the more the tenant mix, and therefore, rent can be maximised. It is, for instance, important in shopping centres to refresh the tenant mix with the strongest line-up, i.e. what shoppers want, or remove underpaying tenants in general.

Operational performance insight: Does the landlord have insight into the operational performance of the tenant? For example, it is especially important for a mall, care home or hotel owner to have insight into the operational performance of the operators. If operations do not go well, rents cannot rise or will not be paid at all. If the operational performance is flagging, landlords can propose changes to the tenant or anticipate a potential bankruptcy.

Lease length: The average lease length is around 5 years these days, but this has come down significantly over the years (it used to be closer to 10 years), although there is a wide range from fully flexible leases to 25-year terms (or even longer). Sometimes real estate owners operate the business themselves, e.g. in the case of hotels and storage. They have short-term contracts with their clientele and can adjust pricing quickly to benefit from positive trends, but the opposite is also often true. The landlords themselves take care of the operations, marketing and (daily) price setting, which requires continuous monitoring of competitors and trends that can affect demand. For example, an event such as a football match, concert or the Olympics can lead to a surge in the search for hotel rooms, and therefore, the price would have to be adjusted quickly, otherwise rooms are being sold too cheaply. Revenue management is a full-time job and normally these companies have teams focused on it. They would need to understand their pricing power; e.g. hotels typically experience more pricing power once occupancy is above 70%, while for storage it is from around 90%.

Be Careful of the Zig-Zag Effect

One of my first lessons in real estate was what I call the 'Zig-Zag' effect. It was when I started to look at offices in Brussels, which offered long leases of up to 25 years to high credit quality tenants such as governments (because the EU has its headquarters there) and annual lease indexation linked to inflation. At first sight, these offices looked like an amazing inflation hedge, but they were not – when the rents expired, the rental income would plummet to the market rent, which typically had not changed much over the years. Clearly, Brussels offices were not a winning sector, i.e. weak underlying fundamentals. As a result, all the growth achieved over the length of the contract through indexation was lost once the contract expired and you would be back to square one. A long rental contract indexed to inflation is not always a true inflation hedge. The underlying supply/demand fundamentals need to be carefully checked, as well as the cost of repositioning the building at the end of the contract.

Table 2.2 shows the difference in internal rate of return (IRR) between two buildings with full annual indexation, but where the second one is reset to the unchanged market rent in year 10. Assuming annual rental indexation of 2.5% and a valuation yield of 5%, the IRR difference is 2% (IRR of 7.5% versus 5.5%; ignoring capex), which is huge and destroys the whole investment case.

(Continued)

(Continued)

Table 2.2 The zig-zag effect

Rents at 2.5% indexation p.a.

Year	1	2	3	4	5	6	7	8	9	10	11	IRR at 5.0% exit yield
Full indexation	100	103	105	108	110	113	116	119	122	125	128	7.5%
Zig-Zag	100	103	105	108	110	113	116	119	122	125	**100**	**5.5%**

Source: Author.

Reversionary Potential

If a tenant is paying more than the market rent, the building has negative rent reversion (it is over-rented). Conversely, if the tenant is paying less, the property has positive reversionary potential (under-rented). Positive reversionary potential indicates good rental growth prospects, and ideally, this should be captured as soon as possible.

Tenant Health

The financial health of the occupier is hugely important in order to drive rental growth but also to make sure the tenant keeps paying the rent in an economic downturn. There can be a long lease, but if the tenant is not financially healthy, they will not pay one day. There have been several insolvency cases, e.g. in the healthcare and retail sectors.

Regulation

The analysis may show that supply/demand fundamentals are strong for a certain type of property, but if rents cannot be raised because of government regulation, the investment case can fall apart. This is particularly an issue in many European residential markets, most notably Germany, where governments set rental levels or rules for future growth. Governments can also have an impact in different ways, e.g. to require a certain level of energy efficiency or loosening/restricting building permits.

Minimum Capital Expenditure and Incentives

Capturing rental growth should be achieved with minimum capex and tenant incentives. For example, landlords might spend on upgrading the building, facilities or infrastructure or induce the tenant to take space, e.g. offering a rent-free period or paying for their fit-out. Shopping centres in the UK have seen a sharp rise in capex and incentives, reaching a point where landlords were spending a lot only to stand still (no rental growth). This is an important piece of the analysis and is often overlooked or underestimated, especially for offices. Capex can 'kill' a potential investment.

Capex

There are different types of capex to consider when owning a property. There is recurring (operating/maintenance) capex, e.g. replacing a broken door handle; one-off capex, e.g. a new lift; tenant capex, e.g. to fit out their space; replacement/obsolescence capex at the end of a rental contract or the building's lifetime; and green capex to update the property for energy consumption and carbon emissions. These different types of capex tend to be underestimated in the underwriting of an investment, especially in bull markets – the 'everything is great and will remain great' mentality – and for lower quality, secondary real estate where the amount of capex is relatively high as a percentage of the value of the asset. In addition, changing tenant requirements, often driven by technology trends, can result in faster building obsolescence and higher than expected capex.

Green Capex

Green capex is relatively new. The EU has been at the forefront in fighting climate change and is committed to reducing greenhouse gas (GHG) emissions by at least 55% by 2030 compared to 1990. As the property sector is responsible for over one-third of global GHG emissions, real estate owners must upgrade their portfolios, i.e. spend on green capex.

Green capex is increasingly having a big impact on occupational and investment markets, as tenants increasingly require 'green' buildings. As a result, 'green' buildings achieve superior rental levels and valuations, whilst out-of-date properties realise significantly lower levels of tenant and investment interest or none at all. Additionally, lenders are increasingly reluctant to provide debt for these outdated properties, whilst offering discounts for 'green' real estate.

This is a real issue, as for some buildings the costs will be too high to bring them up to date, whilst for others the landlord might lack the resources to do the job. A large number of buildings are becoming obsolete with significant drops in value as a result; think 50% or more. Therefore, it is key to have a grip on the portfolio quality before an investment is made. Landlords, on the other hand, should sell as soon as possible if upgrading the assets is too expensive and the opportunity is there. Furthermore, they should carefully assess when to invest in their portfolio if they plan to keep the properties for the long term. Upgrading the assets now would have a positive impact on the asset today, but at a potentially high cost, whilst investing at a later stage might be cheaper due to technological development.

Tenant Incentives

When I started in real estate, I quickly discovered that landlords do not like reducing the rent. Instead, they would much rather keep the same rent but give a rent-free period, e.g. a couple of months to a year on a five-year contract or help with the fitting out of the premises. Whilst it does make sense to support a business in the beginning, all these incentives can cloud the transparency in the market and can subsequently result in unjustified high asset appraisals or overstating the real cash potential of an asset. Moreover, it has happened that a tenant went bankrupt after a lengthy rent-free period, leaving the landlord without pay.

Chapter 3

Scan for Value Add Potential

The most successful investments have an additional value add or growth angle to further boost returns. This requires a deep understanding of the occupier market. The most common ways to create additional value are as follows.

Refurbishment, Extension and Alternative Use

A landlord should investigate whether the property's return can be enhanced through refurbishment. Toby Courtauld, CEO of London office player GPE, says: 'Always create the best quality space. Go for the best; the customer will pay for it. This has never been more true than today'. In addition, a landlord should always consider whether it is possible to extend the property, e.g. by adding a floor or change its use, such as converting an office into residential. These approaches can extract significant value.

Cluster or Platform Creation

Property investors can create significant additional value by assembling a cluster of properties or a platform through which improved pricing power, cost synergies, reduced borrowing costs and development potential can be achieved. Frequently, the destination or platform is branded, such as Silicon Roundabout (East London Tech City) or Shurgard (a storage platform). Shaftesbury Capital deserves a special mention. It acquired properties shop by shop in central London from 1986 to the present day and is now the landlord of significant clusters and entire streets, e.g. Chinatown and Carnaby Street. The company has created a portfolio that is irreplaceable.

Development

Property development can be an effective way to create premium products with attractive returns. Profit margins are typically around 15–20% (the value of the finished building versus the cost to build it) but can reach 50% to even 100% in bull markets. However, development requires skill: a vision, an eye for profitability, creativity, diligent execution and strong risk management. As the well-known Mike Slade, former CEO of London office company Helical Bar, once said to me: 'We all want to build a big penis into the sky, but it is bloody risky!'

Many Developers Struggle During Downturns

Numerous developers encounter serious trouble when a downturn hits because:

- Their revenue plummets, as there are no or limited project sales, because the transaction market has come to a standstill.
- Overhead and debt costs continue to drain cash flows.
- The land bank drops in value, as land prices are highly cyclical.

As a result, developers often run into cash flow and debt covenant issues during a real estate slump. Problems can escalate rapidly, particularly for developers with large (illiquid) land banks and construction projects combined with significant amounts of debt. This was the case in the most recent 2022–2024 downturn with Austrian developer Signa and Chinese developer Evergrande.

Be Careful with Companies Undertaking their First Development Projects

When companies suddenly venture into real estate development, caution is necessary. Firstly, they are likely doing this because the market is too hot to purchase yielding (let) assets, which indicates the market's state. Secondly, I do not know any company that started development without making mistakes: cost overruns and timing delays are very common. This can be extremely costly for development. Remember, this is not within their current expertise. Experienced developers need to be recruited, and the company needs to understand and control the new risks that come with it, such as setting a conservative budget, cost and timing control, focus on pre-letting and leverage. Thirdly, developers tend to fall in love with their projects, losing sight of profitability. I have witnessed a complete blind eye when market conditions change, which means a strong CEO, CFO, and board are required to continuously monitor the situation. All in all, development is a specialised skill.

Acquisitions and Disposals

Acquisitions and disposals are clear ways to create value and optimise a portfolio, although one should always consider the rather high transfer taxes in most countries (typically 5–10%). Acquisitions should not only be well-researched, but it is also important to have a clear view of the future exit strategy. Who would buy it? Property is illiquid, and it is easy to get stuck with an asset. Sometimes, selling the building in pieces can create superior value, such as with a large apartment block. Selling unit by unit is called privatisation, which is essentially the opposite of creating a platform. The asset should be optimised before disposal in terms of tenant line-up and lease length.

Services

Real estate owners can provide services for a fee to third parties, such as property and asset management and development activities, to reduce costs through economies of scale or risk, but it is fair to say this is often not a game changer. Landlords can also operate services in their buildings, such as a coffee bar, to improve the occupier experience.

A Simple Way to Add Value

Andrew Coombs, CEO of Sirius Real Estate, says: 'When we purchase a site, the seller has often not updated the measurements on the floor plan of the property, whilst it has typically been extended over time. Simply by measuring the site ourselves before acquisition, we can often find up to an average of 10% extra space compared to the marketing brochure'.

Chapter 4

Real Estate Is Cyclical

Booms happen, but so do busts. When downturns occur, it is not unheard of for assets to fall 40–50% in value, land by 75%, and, of course, with leverage, the equity drops even faster. From 12 March 2003, European listed real estate stocks staged a huge rally of 284% to the peak of 19 February 2007, after which they fell 77% as a result of the Global Financial Crisis (GFC) to their low on 9 March 2009, i.e. 8% below the start of the rally after the dot-com bubble. The GFC was a nightmare for many landlords. Property values fell sharply, lenders aggressively tried to get their money back and owners were forced to sell assets or issue equity at punitive pricing to shore up their balance sheets, if their equity was not wiped out in the meantime. It takes time for pricing to find a new market equilibrium and for the market to work itself through the deleveraging process. Mike Slade encapsulated this sentiment during the GFC, saying to me, 'I am going to relax. I am not going to do anything for two years'. Real estate is cyclical, although the degree of cyclicality varies by sector and over time. Downturns will come and take time, but the bounce will come too. As a result, downturns can be a perfect moment to invest and to go 'contrarian'.

Warning Signs

A downturn can always happen, e.g. triggered by external events, as we have seen over the years, e.g. COVID-19 and geopolitical tensions, oversupply and monetary tightening. However, there are also some warning signs that can be monitored, to determine whether we are getting closer to a new downturn.

Eight Years after Last Downturn

The long-term real estate index of listed UK real estate stocks has seen three significant downturns since 1965. In the 1970s, it hit a low on 25 November 1974, with stocks down 75% from their high on 6 November 1973. In the 1990s, the low was on 10 September 1992, with stocks down 41% from 5 September 1989. In the first decade of the 21st century, the low was on 9 March 2009, with stocks down 81% from 3 January 2007. Historically, downturns have hit every 8–9 years. The typical pattern was a slowdown, followed by a deep crisis, another slowdown and then another deep crisis. A big crisis happened every 16–18 years.

This is, of course, no guarantee for the future, as other forces are also at work, such as negative structural trends (where these sectors are unlikely to recover) and some researchers claiming the existence of super cycles up to 50–100 years long. However, it keeps investors alert.

I like to monitor the three-year rolling return of the UK property stock index, which seems to show this pattern (Figure 4.1). For example,

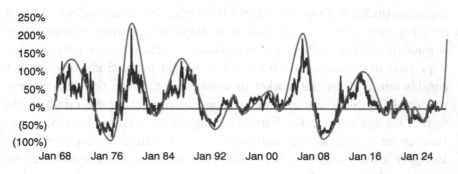

Figure 4.1 EPRA UK – total real return three-year rolling (since 28 January 1968).
Source: Based on data from EPRA, companies, Office for National Statistics.

it seems to indicate that returns should improve from here (September 2024), before a new downturn hits.

DCFM Is Stretched

A simple look at a Discounted Cash Flow Model (DCFM) can help to judge whether a certain investment or market as a whole is coming to its bull (or bear) market end. In my experience, the variables in a DCFM get stretched first (often to the maximum) before the situation changes, typically by an unforeseen event. For example, the exact start date of the GFC was hard to time, if not impossible, but at that time we did know that all the DCFM input variables were significantly stretched versus their long-term average: assumed discount rates, exit cap rates and cost of borrowing were all below their long-term average, expected capital expenditure on the property was typically ignored and expected rental growth was above long-term growth rates. It does not get much better than that!

Real estate is cyclical. Fortunes will change. So, it did that time. Values started to fall and only began to bottom out when all the earlier mentioned variables had moved significantly in the opposite direction! I find this simple check a very helpful tool to judge how far we still have to go or to assess how risky a certain investment is. Table 4.1 shows my assessment of how stretched the DCFM variables were just before the GFC and at its GFC low.

Table 4.1 DCF check (1 loose to 10 stretched)

	At peak	At bottom
Rental growth expectations	9	1
Initial yield	10	1
Exit rate	9	2
Cost of debt	8	4
Cost of equity	9	2
Capex	9	2
% Variables DCF priced in	**90%**	**20%**

Source: Author.

Bubble Symptoms

Additionally, a 'bubble check list' (Table 4.2) is very helpful when things have really gone out of control, as they did in 2006. The market might

42 REAL ESTATE RULES

Table 4.2 Bubble check list

Prices risen rapidly?	☐
Low quality IPOs?	☐
High expectations for continued price growth?	☐
Overvaluation versus historical averages? DCF stretched?	☐
Monetary expansion?	☐
Scandals?	☐
Stock market bubble preceded jump in property prices?	☐
Return expectations have changed?	☐
Price increases in excess of CPI for years?	☐
Price increases boil over to other (sub-)markets?	☐
High expectations?	☐
Other parties/speculative buyers joined the scene?	☐
Insiders negative?	☐
Direct market pricing irrational?	☐
Stock market pricing irrational?	☐

Source: Adapted from *Bubbles and How to Survive Them* (London: Nicholas Brealey, 2004).

not only look fully priced, but may also be driven to irrational levels by speculative buyers, extremely high expectations (forever...), and loose monetary policy. Furthermore, insiders (property 'gurus') might be selling out, scandals (e.g. fraud) appearing and low-quality initial public offerings (IPOs) being brought to the stock exchange – all of which were the case in 2006. Many boxes were ticked on the bubble check list.

The opposite also happens. When I started as an analyst in 2001, not many people cared about listed real estate. The sector was completely out of favour. All the attention was on technology, media and telecoms (TMT). These periods occur from time to time: investors see better returns in other equity sectors and ignore real estate, which can sometimes result in significant discounts for property stocks versus their intrinsic value. But one should have bought property at that time: a massive rally was on its way. It is often the case that one bubble pops, but another bubble appears somewhere else. In this case, it moved from the internet to property, as shown in Figure 4.2 of the Nasdaq versus the real estate benchmark EPRA Europe index.

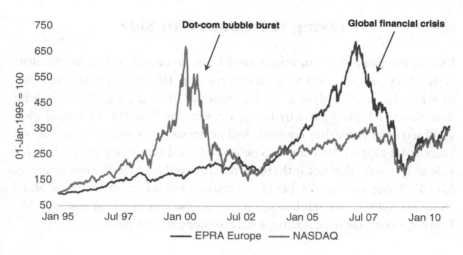

Figure 4.2 EPRA Europe versus NASDAQ – total return
Source: FactSet.

Fly Me to the Moon ... and Back ...

In 2014, the flexible office concept was in vogue, with many companies presenting business cases with unlimited growth at extremely high valuations. All these providers tried to copy the US company WeWork Inc., which was growing fast. WeWork provides coworking spaces, including physical and virtual shared spaces. It rents office space from landlords and leases the space to third parties (individuals, small businesses and larger companies) by offering more trendy spaces, services and flexible contracts. WeWork became a hype, which would not end well.

We received several proposals to invest, but these were generally businesses with not much substance yet – a couple of flexible offices with a business plan that predicted more than doubling earnings every year for the next 10 years. Businesses were loss-making today, but were forecast to make enormous profits from year five onwards. If one pumps infinite growth at an extraordinary rate into a discounted cash flow (DCF) valuation model with limited investment, one arrives at an amazing blue-sky valuation. Clearly, this was not something for us, as it was not sustainable, but it was interesting to follow nonetheless!

Taking the Contrarian Side

One of the things I continuously hear from successful real estate investors is that they are prepared to go contrarian, i.e. take the opposite position of what the 'market flavour of the moment' is, and go (all) in. Sir John Templeton achieved fame by being a contrarian investor: he would look at which sectors (within equities) had performed poorly over the last five years. If he judged the reason to be of a cyclical nature, he would buy (or at least not sell). But not if there were structural reasons. Within property, Sam Zell was famous for being contrarian. He wrote in his book *Am I Being Too Subtle?*: 'My tendency is to go against conventional wisdom'.[1] In Europe, Yakir Gabay is, for me, a success story in real estate.

First in Berlin

Gabay is a self-made man, who epitomises success in European real estate. He started in Israel in investment banking and asset management, but it truly kicked off in 2004, when Gabay and his lawyer attended property auctions in Berlin. He was the only bidder. At that time only few investors were interested in investing in Germany, but based on Gabay's assessment, it was cheap on all metrics: 'A deal should work on its own not assuming on purely riding a cycle'. He acted on his contrarian view and went all in with conviction. He purchased his first residential property for €1 million: 33 large apartments in the centre of Berlin at a price of €200 per sq. m, while it would have cost €1,500 per sq. m at the time to construct the building; the so-called replacement cost. The starting yield on the acquisition was 10%, with an initial vacancy rate of 30%. It would turn out to be a great deal: today, on my calculations, the property would be more than 10 times as expensive, and the original rent more than quadrupled through filling up the building vacancy and rent increases. In the second half of 2005, Irish investors started to arrive at the auctions and by 2006 the room was full. Germany was in vogue.

Gabay did not only focus on residential real estate, but also on hotels, where he found attractive deals too. For instance, he bought a hotel at one point for €1 as the owner thought the capital expenditure would be exceedingly high and was keen to get rid of the running costs of a closed building. He turned it around. Gabay did not have sufficient capital to exploit every opportunity and therefore set up partnerships with other equity investors. He would put in 25% of the equity, other investors putting up the rest, plus financial leverage. For some deals, before the GFC, banks were prepared to give more than 90% leverage. That is huge. This amount of leverage meant that the return to Gabay and his partners would be multiplied by 10. So, if a return of 100% was made (not unheard of at that time), the return would be a whopping 1,000% for them! In addition, Gabay would receive 50% of the profit above a certain rate of return, also called the hurdle rate.

Having the market timing spot on, combined with creative financing, a high level of diligence and a strong eye for value creation, Gabay's money machine was born. He had a keen eye for finding undervalued and under-managed portfolios, e.g. from banks, receivers, distressed owners and court auctions, which he managed to turn around with his team. In 2007, he had a major exit to Lehman Brothers real estate fund, which was a perfect timing to realise his profits. In 2010, he went on to found German residential real estate company Grand City Properties, which listed on the Frankfurt Stock Exchange in 2012. In 2015, he created the listed company Aroundtown (AT1), as he also saw an opportunity in German offices.

What Not to Do – Anecdote by Toby Courtauld

'One of the first buildings we bought, since I became the CEO of GPE, was the Met building in 2003 (22 Percy Street near Tottenham Court Road, London). We paid £16 million, less than £200 psf [per square foot] and refurbished it for £23.8 million. In August 2007 it was sold to Lazari Investments for £107 million. In 2009 I called Christos Lazari, hoping we could purchase the building back on the cheap, but Lazari Investments was not distressed and Christos was very displeased with my call. We never spoke again'. (Note: Christos Lazari passed away in 2015.)

Note

1. Sam Zell (2017) *Am I being too subtle?* (New York: Penguin Random House), p. 27.

Chapter 5

Expected Returns Should Beat Cost of Capital

After the previous rules have been properly analysed, the key question is at what level it would be interesting to purchase or sell a certain asset. Would the investment generate a strong total return for the coming years or are expected returns poor? Or if the property is no longer the building of the future, e.g. because of a technology change, will it continue to decline in value? Critical analysis is key to avoid investing in underperforming real estate, or worse, in properties that are in terminal decline.

The ultimate goal is to identify properties that will produce strong returns above the required return, i.e. have a relatively high yield, low rental levels (by historical standards), strong fundamentals for rental growth, a price per square metre (price psm) significantly below replacement value and modest capital expenditure (capex) requirements. The opposite, i.e. a low yield, high rent, weak rental growth outlook, price

47

psm above replacement value and high capex, indicates the asset should not be bought or is long overdue to be sold. Investing should be based on multicriteria valuations and contain a significant margin for error.

Whilst this is not a book with detailed valuation models, it will give some basic guidance.

Yield and Price per Square Metre

There are two easy-to-calculate valuation metrics. Both can be used in their own way, but also compared to recent and historical transaction evidence of similar properties.

Yield: We earlier saw a range of different types of yield calculations in Chapter 1. All these yields add some value, but I prefer the European Public Real Estate Association (EPRA) net yield and the EPRA topped-up yield as a starting point for the valuation analysis. Note that the yield formula (rent divided by value) can be rearranged in a simple formula to calculate the value of an asset: value = rent divided by yield, where 'rent' is the same rent as used to calculate the yield.

Price per square metre (price psm) or price per square foot in the UK (price psf): This is simply calculated as the value of the building divided by the square metres of the floor area or usable space. Ideally, the price psm is below the replacement value, so that a developer cannot build a cheaper building next door. It indicates that rents have to grow first before competing properties arise. The replacement value is the value of the land plus today's cost to construct the building, divided by the area. Construction costs for residential and office buildings tend to be in the range of €2,500–€4,000 psm depending on the sector or location.

Recall that a high yield and a low price psm do not necessarily mean that it is a great purchase. It can also be a dying asset. The metrics should be evaluated per sector and location, and in terms of their rental growth prospects.

Expected Return

The expected return of the asset can be calculated using a Discounted Cash Flow Model (DCFM) for a five-year period. A longer period may

Expected Returns Should Beat Cost of Capital 49

be chosen if there are significant value drivers beyond this horizon, but longer periods are more susceptible to forecast errors.

I will not display a detailed DCFM here, but instead focus on the long-term version of it. It is a simple equation, but uses three key variables for an easy and quick analysis. The aim is to find an asset with high yield and high expected portfolio rental growth, e.g. because there are strong underlying demand/supply fundamentals, at a minimal capex cost. It is especially easy to use for properties with a predictable rental growth profile.

$$Expected\ Return = Yield + Expected\ Medium\text{-}Term\ Rental$$
$$Growth - Capex \tag{5.1}$$

(all expressed as %)

Yield is the EPRA net initial yield. The *Expected Medium-Term Rental Growth* is estimated on a like-for-like basis, i.e. assuming an unchanged portfolio composition, over the upcoming five years. *Capex* is the annualised cost to maintain the portfolio in a good state in the longer term, which has not yet been reflected in the *Yield* yet. It is expressed as a percentage of the value of the asset.

It is best to calculate ungeared returns first. Leverage can be added as a second layer to enhance profits if the investment case is strong.

Beat the Cost of Capital

Next, it is crucial to understand whether the expected return is higher than the required return, also known as the weighted average cost of capital (WACC). The WACC is calculated as follows:

$$WACC = Weighted\ Average\ Cost\ of\ Debt$$
$$+ Weighted\ Average\ Cost\ of\ Equity \tag{5.2}$$

It is important to note that the WACC is based on today's cost of debt and today's cost of equity, with their weightings determined by a company's target capital structure rather than its current structure. Continuous monitoring of financial markets is essential to calculate these variables. For instance, I track the five-year swap rate (a key rate for real estate) plus the margin and other costs applied by banks to determine the cost of debt. I also regularly consult with chief financial officers (CFOs) of real estate companies to understand the rates offered by debt providers. Additionally, I keep an eye on public bond markets for real-time pricing of outstanding bonds.

For the cost of equity, I use the Capital Asset Pricing Model (CAPM). According to CAPM, the required return on equity equals the risk-free rate (I use the 10-year government bond yield) plus a risk premium. The risk premium is determined by the company's beta multiplied by a market risk premium. As a rule of thumb, a beta of 1 indicates that the company's share price moves in line with the general equity index. A beta less than 1 suggests less volatility than the index, while a beta greater than 1 indicates higher volatility. Typically, the beta for the real estate sector is below 1, with residential properties at the lower end and commercial real estate at the higher end (offices are today >1), depending on factors such as the quality of the real estate and the stage of the economic cycle. I set the market risk premium at 5%, consistent with its long-term average ranging between 4.5% and 5%.

The WACC calculation may seem complex initially, but once understood – including how these variables behave – it can be easily calculated, monitored and updated. In my experience, the WACC for an average real estate portfolio tends to be around 7% over the long term. Higher-quality assets and residential properties often have WACCs closer to 6%, while developments or assets in less developed countries may require a return around 10%.

In step 3 of the analysis, we compare the expected return (1) with the WACC (2):

$$\text{Expected Return} - \text{WACC} \qquad (5.3)$$

If the expected return exceeds the WACC, it suggests that forecast returns are 'healthy': assets are likely to attract more aggressive buyers willing to pay higher prices, thereby reducing the yield and bringing the expected return closer to the WACC. Conversely, if the expected return falls below the WACC, it indicates insufficient forecast returns, potentially causing yields to widen by the difference between the WACC and the expected return. Values are anticipated to decline. It is a quick way to make an assessment of a property valuation.

Expected Returns Should Beat Cost of Capital

These three simple formulas have been invaluable in quickly assessing both market and specific company situations. For instance, in 2022, when the WACC for German residential companies surged from around 4% at the start of the year to approximately 6% by mid-year, with limited expected compensation from increased medium-term rental growth due to government regulations, the formulas suggested that yields should increase by over 1 percentage point. Given that yields on German residential properties were low at 3%, a rise to 4% implied that values could plummet by 25%. Considering the average loan-to-value ratio was 43% for these stocks, implying a leverage multiplier of 1.75, equity valuations would be impacted by over 40%! This significant negative impact stemmed from low property yields and relatively high leverage.

Furthermore, such valuation declines indicated that some German residential companies might face issues with their debt covenants, potentially shifting from buyers to sellers of real estate. A dividend cut and, at worst, an equity issuance at a depressed price were also possible outcomes. It's no surprise that stock volatility was high (daily movements exceeding 4% were common), particularly amidst uncertain economic prospects and fluctuating interest rates/bond yields.

Another example occurred in 2009 during the aftermath of the Global Financial Crisis (GFC), when I was an analyst at JP Morgan. Central banks had initiated various programmes to lower capital costs through interest rate reductions and quantitative easing to stimulate bank lending and economic growth. Despite the prevailing uncertainty, the listed space began to appear attractive as many companies had strengthened their balance sheets, and the expected return (under conservative assumptions) was more than 1% higher than the WACC. This insight prompted me to upgrade stocks and advocate their potential.

Conservative Underwriting

Given real estate is cyclical and setbacks can happen (e.g. a tenant going bust), it is important to invest based on a conservative underwriting, i.e. include a margin for error and run various potential future scenarios beforehand: a bear/base/bull case with different rental growth and cost of capital assumptions. Clearly, it is ideal when an investment case 'works' even with a high margin for error and bear case scenario. Jamie Ritblat, chairman and founder of Delancey, said: 'Invest for rainy days, the sunshine will take care of itself'.

Act!

If the expected return significantly exceeds the required return and there is a clear expectation of future buyers (liquidity upon exit), investors should consider acquiring the asset. It is a good habit to monitor which sectors the major real estate players, such as leading private equity firms like Blackstone and Brookfield, are directing their capital towards.

When the analysis signals a Sell recommendation, landlords should consider divesting the asset, especially if it is considered a 'dry' asset. Guillaume Poitrinal, former CEO of Unibail-Rodamco and my current business partner, said:

> At Unibail-Rodamco [now URW], we evaluated each holding annually. In our 5-year budget-plan exercise, every asset was assumed to be sold at appraised value. It is only if we could demonstrate a double digit annual IRR (pre-tax, pre-leverage) starting from the latest appraised value that the disposal would not be engaged into. If not put for sale, the asset was simulated to be bought again, at appraised value. And we would start a new 5-year value creation process. Keeping core assets for eternity may appear safe investments but is actually high-risk due to interest rate sensitivity, but also to mere obsolescence of the properties. Agility is king. Don't sleep on your assets.

Some investors develop emotional attachments to their assets, even when circumstances have deteriorated. Andrew Jones, who successfully transitioned the company from retail property to logistics by attentively listening to the tenants, stated: 'Many real estate executives suffer from what's known as Stockholm syndrome. They become too attached to their assets, marrying the problem and failing to anticipate shifts in direction'. While some retail property landlords took action, others remained in denial for extended periods. One CEO famously asserted: 'You can't buy a suit on the internet'.

Other landlords reach the correct conclusion but opt not to sell, fearing short-term earnings impact. However, delaying a sale often results in lower valuations and greater income loss over time. It's crucial to focus on total return (yield and valuation growth). Some companies do sell but advertise it too publicly, harming the potential sale price, as buyers know they have committed themselves. Failing to sell would result in losing face publicly.

Investment Practices: Then Versus Now

When I was a property analyst 20 years ago, I went on an asset inspection trip. The CEO welcomed me, saying, 'Hi Harm, nice to see you here! It is also my first time seeing the asset!' The asset was a significant investment for the company and only a 30-minute drive from his office. It turned out to be a disastrous acquisition. While common practice today, many companies at the time did not conduct sophisticated analyses, let alone calculate an internal rate of return (IRR) or create annual business plans for each asset. This often resulted in disastrous purchases or sticking to underperforming assets for far too long. Today, the investment underwriting process is generally more professional than it was in the past.

Chapter 6

Central Bank and Government Stimuli (or Lack of) Can Be Game Changers

Central banks (through monetary policy) and governments (through taxes, regulation and policies) can stimulate or break an investment case. In particular, central banks have played a major role in real estate markets over the years.

The mentioned formulas in the previous chapter can be very helpful in assessing the impact of these stimuli, which can be immense. For example, if the central bank reduces the cost of capital from 7% to 6%, the expected return will also fall by 1%, as buyers will continue to bid prices

55

upwards as long as the expected return is higher or equal to the cost of capital. Assuming everything else remains equal and the original yield on a property was 5%, it will now fall to 4%, boosting property values by 25% (5% divided by 4% − 1) and the equity by a whopping 50%, if the loan-to-value ratio is 50% (2× multiplier).

In September 2009, I argued in a report titled 'Castles Made of Sand', in my role as a real estate analyst at JP Morgan, that future profits were being front-loaded by central banks and that the situation did not look sustainable in the long term. Real estate markets were heavily supported by money printing from central banks, with Fed Chairman Ben Bernanke often being referred to as 'Helicopter Ben', which made me frequently assess the risk of hyperinflation. Over the years, I repeatedly wondered whether this would end well. Many market participants knew that this stimulation would not last forever, but the overriding comment was: 'If the goal posts get moved to another field, stop arguing whether that was right or not, just move to the other field and start scoring goals!'

During the COVID-19 period (2020–2022), the stimuli reached another dimension. Not only did central banks go all in, with the Bank of England (BoE) cutting its base rate from 0.75% to 0.1% and the European Central Bank (ECB) maintaining its all-time low deposit rate of −0.50%, but also extensive support programmes were launched. For example, the ECB stated it would do everything necessary to defend the Euro area and launched a €1,850 billion pandemic emergency purchase programme (PEPP) aimed at lowering borrowing costs and increasing lending in the Euro area. Additionally, governments joined in and spent billions and billions with no limits. According to the National Audit Office, the COVID response cost the UK a staggering £376 billion, which was 16% of the total outstanding debt of £2,365 billion at the end of Q1 2022. Interestingly, the COVID response cost was significantly higher than the cost of 'making the UK green'. The Office for Budget Responsibility estimated around that time that the net cost of the UK reaching net zero by 2050 would be £321 billion.

In the end, all these stimuli boosted real estate markets for approximately 14 years until they had to be gradually withdrawn, starting in 2022 due to spiking inflation. The 'Castles Made of Sand' were finally washed away, with one of the biggest real estate beneficiaries of loose monetary conditions, German residential properties, losing all their share price gains.

German Residential Implosion

The implosion of the German residential property market exemplified the effects of first a loose and then the normalisation of monetary policy. German residential players saw returns of 278% from the beginning of 2014 until their peak in August 2021, equating to an annualised return of almost 20%. Net property yields steadily fell by 3 percentage points (to below 3% in certain cities such as Berlin), rents steadily rose and additional gains were made through refurbishments and development. Many companies aggressively purchased portfolios by increasing financial leverage, often booking immediate valuation gains, a phenomenon known as the Lucky Buyer effect.

The Lucky Buyer effect is controversial. On one hand, it can be argued that management did a great job by acquiring portfolios off-market at a discount, but on the other hand, it raises the question of why someone would sell at a discount. Nevertheless, due to the end of loose monetary policy in 2022/2023, the stocks fell by more than 65%. In the first half of 2023, share prices of German residential companies, such as Vonovia, fell back to their 2014 levels, leaving an annualised return of just below 3% from dividends (Figure 6.1). German residential property was particularly hard hit because of its low cash flow yield, high levels of financial leverage (both the result of the booming years) and regulated rents. Finally, what I saw as confirmation of the end of a boom was the emergence of scandals, e.g. with the Adler Group, which I discuss in Chapter 19 in detail.

It is important to follow, analyse and understand central banks and governments. The key takeaways of the last few years are as follows.

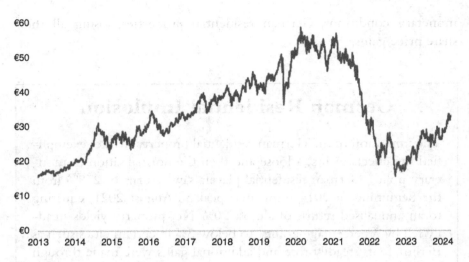

Figure 6.1 Vonovia share price
Source: FactSet.

Central Banks Tend to Get Their Way

When central banks are determined to stimulate or restrict, one better takes note. Most often, it is better not to fight them, as they have the power to change the rules of the game. It is crucial to understand their thinking: what are they focused on? Saving the property market? Reducing inflation? Decreasing unemployment? Markets can create noise and overshoot, but always keep in mind what the central banks aim to achieve. The same can be said about governments. For example, numerous housing markets are susceptible to increased government regulation, if they become overheated.

Engineered Volatility, but …

Once the central bank's path is clear to the market, the volatility of investment returns will fall, but it will come back with a vengeance. For example, during the period of loose monetary policy, yields on some types of real estate fell significantly from 7% to even 3%, generating a value increase of 133% from the yield change alone! However, a property valued at a 3% yield is much more sensitive to an interest rate change than one at 7%, thereby increasing the sector's risk profile. If the yield were to increase by 1% from 7%, the value would fall by 12.5% (7% divided by 8% − 1), whereas the value would fall by 25% (twice as much) for a move from 3% to 4% (3% divided by 4% − 1).

Bail Out if 'Majority Is in Trouble'

Governments and central banks are highly likely to step in and bail out if the 'majority is in trouble'. For example, during the Global Financial Crisis, many individual property owners were too highly leveraged, but central banks helped them out by lowering interest rates. While this intervention was understandable, it created a moral hazard situation. As a result, overgeared investors got bailed out, whilst it was still difficult for cautious individuals to enter the housing market.

However, do not expect large real estate owners to be bailed out by default, especially not by governments, who are more voter-focused and often target real estate for charges, particularly as the asset cannot be moved. For example, during COVID, many policies aimed at supporting people and their businesses but offered no assistance to shopping centres. In fact, it was considered acceptable not to pay rent.

Stimulus or Restrictive Policy Will End One Day

Divergence from the long-term average or historically ultra-loose/strict monetary policies will eventually revert. Be prepared for this when investing. Ensure that the cost of capital in your underwriting is sustainable and not temporarily engineered. As mentioned earlier, allow a margin for error in your investment by using a higher WACC when monetary conditions are loose, assuming it can return to the long-term average. Additionally, seek compensation through value-add strategies and the ability to increase rental growth in different economic scenarios, ensuring strong underlying market fundamentals.

Arbitrage Opportunities Opening Up

Certain sectors, countries and cities may benefit more or less than others. For example, there is one interest rate for all countries in the Euro area,

60   REAL ESTATE RULES

but each country or even city has a different economic growth outlook. Generally, this means that countries or cities with high economic growth will have an interest rate that is too low, while those with low economic growth will have an interest rate that is too high. As a result, the real estate market in the former will be overstimulated, while in the latter, it will be under stimulated.

Part II

Capital Structure

Adding leverage can significantly enhance returns but can also destroy a business. A secure balance sheet is vital: companies should not be caught out in downturns or by black swan events due to high financial leverage, insufficient cash flows to service interest payments, tight debt covenants, large upcoming refinancings or overdependence on a specific debt market (which could be closed). On the contrary, companies should have permanent access to capital markets to seize investment opportunities as they arise. To quote Rogier Quirijns, senior portfolio manager at Cohen & Steers: 'Fear and greed are like the devil on your shoulder. A strong balance sheet is an angel on your shoulder'.

Part II

Capital Structure

Chapter 7

Prudent Use of Financial Leverage: Don't Get Caught Out by Downturns

If one has a strong 'once-in-a-lifetime' conviction, an excellent track record in 'timing the cycle' and can handle the potential loss of all equity, one might decide to leverage to the maximum. In fact, this is how some successful investors have made significant gains. Yakir Gabay said to me, 'Act on conviction, go with full strength when the opportunity is obvious'. However, most investors and in particular large long-term minded companies such as listed REITs need to be more careful with leverage. They can be caught out by downturns as capital and investment markets can close immediately. This results in a dire situation where deleveraging is only possible at a (too) high cost (e.g. dividend cuts, highly dilutive equity issues, deeply discounted disposals or debt at double-digit rates, if available at all), leading to a sliding scale of credit rating downgrades, potential covenant breaches and potential default. Prudent use of leverage is key.

Stay the Course

I will never forget meeting investors in London with Dutch property company Wereldhave at the end of 2006. Its seasoned CEO, Gijs Verweij, who had been with the company for more than 25 years, was criticised at every meeting: 'Why is your leverage so low? Why have you missed the boat? What have you actually done over the last few years?' The prevailing view was that he hadn't done enough and that the company had become a takeover candidate. By the end of the day, the CEO was beaten down and puzzled, doubting his strategy. Had he been too cautious? Was he so wrong? Fortunately, he remained conservative. Soon after, the Global Financial Crisis hit. Wereldhave's share price plummeted by more than 60% from its peak in 2007 to the trough in 2009. With high leverage, it would have been an even bigger disaster.

Capital Markets Do Not Reward High Leverage, the Opposite!

Financial markets generally do not appreciate excessive leverage. For example, shopping centre bellwether Unibail-Rodamco-Westfield (URW) outperformed its peer Klépierre by 76% after the merger with Rodamco in 2007 until it announced the acquisition of Westfield in December 2017. During this period, URW's gearing was significantly lower than Klépierre's (see Figure 7.1). However, the situation completely reversed after the takeover: leverage was now higher, and the cumulative outperformance turned into a cumulative underperformance of 78% (a change of more than 150%!) till end of June 2023. Dirk Philippa, former Head of Global Listed Real Estate Equities at Fidelity International, remarked, 'In the long term, higher financial leverage always leads to underperformance'.

Prudent Use of Financial Leverage

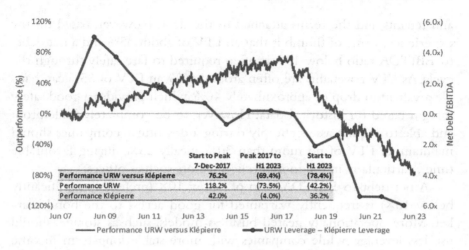

Figure 7.1 URW underperforms when leverage exceeds closest rival
Source: FactSet, annual reports of URW and Klépierre.

Loose or No Covenants

The amount of leverage should be considered in combination with the covenants attached to the debt. Sir John Ritblat, honorary president (and formerly chairman and CEO) of British Land, said, 'It is crucial that you are in a position where the banks cannot get their money back and that you do not need to sell'. Ideally, there would be no loan-to-value (LTV) or interest cover covenants, but also flexibility in other ratios that can make it harder to sell assets. For instance, debt can be secured against properties, but it can also be unsecured, in which case the unencumbered ratio is important – i.e. the ratio of unencumbered properties (those not subject to a creditor's claim) to the amount of unsecured debt or total assets. The lower the minimum of this ratio is set in the debt covenants, the higher the flexibility for the borrower, as more assets can be used for other financial purposes, such as securing new additional loans.

Can Absorb a Value Decline of at Least 40%

The 'optimal' financial leverage varies by subsector, business model, level of dividend distribution, stage of the cycle, quality of the rental contracts and tenants and the terms attached to the debt. However, based on my experience, a rule of thumb is that an LTV of about 35% and a net debt-to-EBITDA ratio below 10× is often required to fare safely through the cycle. As LTV covenants are often around 60%, an LTV of 35% can handle a valuation drop of approximately 40%, which provides a good safety margin based on historical data. However, to be completely bulletproof and able to acquire assets cheaply during a downturn, companies should maintain an LTV of no more than 30%, ideally 25%, during favourable times, particularly in the more cyclical sectors such as offices.

A net debt-to-EBITDA ratio of below 10× (preferably significantly below 10×) is frequently warranted for good access to the bond market. More operationally geared business models, such as storage, should use less leverage, while companies with more stable long-term income can use higher levels. I therefore disagree with market commentators who use these rules too strictly, almost forcing companies to raise equity or sell assets when they are absolutely fine. For example, there is a big difference between an asset with a 25-year government lease annually indexed to inflation versus a tertiary office with a short-term lease in a high vacancy area.

No Endless Leverage on Valuation Gains

However, LTV should be considered in combination with other debt ratios, such as net debt to EBITDA and interest cover,[1] to mitigate the risk of leveraging on valuation gains. Many investors take on more debt when the values of their existing portfolio rise. It can be an easy way to boost earnings, particularly when debt terms are favourable, there is a positive yield spread (between the yield on property and the cost of debt), and sentiment is bullish with ever-rising values. But it decreases the margin for error when a downturn hits. This happens repeatedly with real estate companies. Investors should pay close attention.

Table 7.1 illustrates what typically happens. Initially, the company had an LTV of 50%, which was fair for its business model and the stage of the cycle. Subsequently, real estate entered a boom, resulting in its valuation yield falling from 6% to 4% (called yield compression) and values rising by 50%. Note that whilst the LTV went down to 33%, its net debt-to-EBITDA ratio stayed at 8.3 times, and its interest cover at 3.4 times.

Table 7.1 Example of leveraging up on valuation gains

€m	Initial investment	Valuation increase +50%	Gear-up
Amount purchased			**50**
Value	100	150	200
Net debt	50	50	100
LTV	50%	33%	50%
Yield on property	6.0%	4.0%	4.0%
Cost of debt	3.5%	3.5%	3.5%
EBITDA	6.00	6.00	8.00
Earnings	4.25	4.25	4.50
Net debt to EBITDA	**8.3×**	**8.3×**	**12.5×**
Interest cover	**3.4×**	**3.4×**	**2.3×**

Source: Author.

Now, management decides to gear up on its higher property values by acquiring properties financed with debt, bringing its LTV back to 50% again. In this example, the company purchases another £50 million in real estate, which will increase its recurring earnings by 6% from £4.24 million to £4.5 million. That is typically celebrated and paid out in higher dividends to shareholders, but now its other two debt ratios have worsened as well: the net debt-to-EBITDA ratio has risen to 12.5 times (+50%), and its interest cover has fallen to 2.3 times (−33%). A downturn is not only much more likely after the strong increase in property valuations, but it will also have a more devastating impact than would have been the case without the acquisitions. Additionally, the leverage ratios will deteriorate further when a downturn hits because of falling values (higher LTV) and loss of income, e.g. due to an increase in vacancy and lower rents (higher net debt to EBITDA).

Increasingly Difficult to Degear above 50% LTV

It is crucial to realise that once financial leverage rises to substantial levels, it becomes increasingly hard to reduce debt ratios. Consider this situation: a company needs to reduce its LTV ratio by 10% in the middle of a downturn and would have to accept a significant discount of, say, 20% on property disposals (Figure 7.2). If its LTV ratio is 50%, it would have to sell 25% of the portfolio to reduce the LTV to 40%, which is already a daunting task for a large investment company. At higher leverage levels, it is almost impossible. It would need to sell one-third of the assets if the LTV is 60% and two-thirds with a leverage of 75% (in order to reduce leverage by 10%). At an LTV of 80%, the company would be selling assets merely to cover debt, leaving no equity. This is why financial markets are becoming cautious about companies with an LTV close to 50% and why it becomes very hard to deleverage once leverage starts to rise significantly above this level during adverse market conditions.

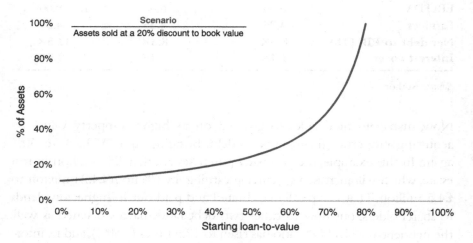

Figure 7.2 Required asset sales to reduce loan-to-value by 10 percentage points
Source: Author.

Success in Lugano – Anecdote by Sir John Ritblat

'In 1972, I asked Rothschild for an unsecured bond, but I was told that we would never get the paper away because I had only started the company a couple of years before. However, Warburg did agree to do the bond issue. We prepared the prospectus and set up a roadshow, which began in Geneva, but there were not many interested investors, even fewer in Zurich, Basel, and Bern. The trip

> was looking like a disaster! Finally, we reached Lugano. Within an hour, the bond was fully subscribed from Italy! It was "hot". I later understood that they thought it was the British Government issuing a (hedged) Swiss-denominated bond. The bond would later collapse, which gave us the opportunity to buy it back for nearly nothing!'

Note

1. Interest cover: the number of times the interest payments are covered by earnings, calculated as EBITDA divided by recurring interest costs.

Chapter 8

Don't Assume That Financing Will Always Be Available

Banks were in trouble during the Global Financial Crisis (GFC). The UK government had to intervene and paid, at its peak, £137 billion in the form of loans and new capital. Banks were no longer open for business; even worse, they wanted to have their money back as soon as possible. As one CEO of a British property company said to me at the time: 'Some banks turned into voracious animals'. Because the bond market was also closed, companies could not rely on debt being available (not even for renewals or extensions), and if debt was available, the terms would be extremely punitive. Investors should take note: do not count on financing to always be there. To eliminate this risk, in addition to a prudent level of financial leverage for Rule 7, the following points are important.

71

Sufficient Cash Flow

The operating cash flow plus available credit lines should cover committed or needed capital expenditure (capex) (e.g. developments but also any acquisitions), debt maturities and dividend payments. Ideally, this should be for a minimum of the next 24 months. If not, significant trouble could be ahead, particularly in the case of a downturn. This happened to the German property company TAG Immobilien in 2022. In December 2021, it announced the purchase of a residential platform in Poland for €550 million, increasing its loan-to-value (LTV) ratio to approximately 45% (a case of gearing up on valuation gains) and planned to sort out the financing later. But then the world changed in the first half of 2022 with the Russia–Ukraine conflict and a sharply rising cost of debt. Its share price slumped from €23 at the time of the acquisition and it was forced to do a €200 million rights issue at €6.90 per share in July 2022. The share price would drop even lower, as market concerns remained about whether enough equity was raised. In December 2022, it hit a low of €5.37, 77% lower than the share price at the time of the acquisition. That was a very expensive Polish transaction.

Spread in Maturities and Lenders

It is important that companies have diversity in their funding: different sources of capital (from lending banks, bond markets, private placements, etc.) and different maturities. Too much dependence on one source or one moment in time can prove disastrous if worse times arrive. For instance, the bond markets tend to close during downturns or become very expensive. This can especially be an issue for large real estate companies if there are doubts about their business model and they need to refinance a couple of billion. Who is going to lend that? If companies are too dependent on one particular bank and need to refinance, trouble could be ahead as well if the lender itself is in difficulties or has become more cautious because of a weakening real estate market.

Equity Should Be Raised When Conditions Are Favourable

Frequently, companies target the almost impossible: raising equity at all-time high valuations in combination with an acquisition. If share prices

Don't Assume That Financing Will Always Be Available   73

are high, it most likely indicates that the underlying property markets are 'hot', so it is not easy to find attractive transactions. And if it is possible to find an acquisition, it is hard to time the closing of the purchase with the date of equity issuance. Instead, ambitious companies with strong management teams should strongly consider raising equity when the markets are open and valuations are reasonable. I am much less enthusiastic about alternative ways of financing, such as through joint ventures (JVs), where another party takes a share of a particular project. These structures are often complicated and add limited value. As a CEO told me: 'The best day of a JV is the day of closing'.

Alternative Financing

There are many different debt or semi-debt/semi-equity products, such as mezzanine, i.e. subordinated debt with an equity component, or hybrid instruments, e.g. convertible bonds, perpetual bonds and preferred shares, which can be used to optimise the finance structure or fill in a gap other capital providers cannot fulfil. Additionally, from time to time, these products can have attractive terms. For example, a number of listed real estate companies issued hybrid bonds (perpetual instruments) when monetary conditions were extremely loose. These instruments were issued at incredibly cheap terms, frequently with a coupon between 1.5% and 3%, so it made complete sense to explore them. However, there is one thing to keep in mind: public markets are lazy. They don't like complexity; they like simplicity. So, whilst these products can be amazing, they are not always properly appreciated by financial markets, as they do not fully understand them. This can result in valuation discounts at times of uncertainty. Companies should take that into consideration.

Good Relationships with Debt Providers

It is crucial to maintain good relationships with the credit rating agencies and debt providers; in other words, don't betray their trust. Their support is essential if troubles arise. For example, if a bank must reduce its exposure to property in a downturn, it should still be willing to lend to your company while cutting off others.

Disagreement

The Nordic real estate company Citycon cancelled its contract with the rating agency Moody's in June 2023, fearing a downgrade to non-investment grade, which it believed would not be a fair assessment. Citycon, on terminating the Moody's contract, stated: 'The termination is a consequence of Moody's current rating methodology, which does not recognise the characteristics of Citycon's tenant mix and business model of creating and operating necessity-based retail hubs in top Nordic locations. The tenant mix of Citycon's assets, comprising municipal and grocery anchor tenants with indexation-linked leases, sets us apart from our peer group and has already demonstrated its strength and resilience in a variety of market conditions'.[1] Nevertheless, Moody's downgraded Citycon shortly thereafter.

Rights Issues Value Destructive in Downturns

Shortage of Capital in Downturns

Some listed companies believe they can always raise equity, no matter the market circumstances, by doing it in the form of a rights issue. This means that, depending on the size of their holding, every shareholder receives a number of rights to buy new shares at an often significantly discounted price. Economic theory indicates that if every investor receives new shares in proportion to their holding at the same discount, it is fine – a zero-sum game. In 'normal' times, this is indeed the case, and a rights issue can be a good way to raise capital. However, this is often not the case in a real estate downturn. It assumes that every shareholder has cash readily available to take up these rights or, if not, can sell them to somebody else at 'fair' value. This is a problem, because in downturns such as the GFC, there is a shortage of capital. Many investors are unable to take up their rights because they don't have the cash available, nor do others. As a result, these rights are traded at lower prices, and investors who do not have the money available lose out. Nowadays, management teams understand this: everything else should be done first – selling assets, cutting costs and potentially cutting the dividend.

The UK Rights Issues at the End of the GFC

At the start of 2009, the listed property sector, particularly in the UK, was in freefall, as market participants were increasingly worried about their balance sheet situation and began to anticipate dilutive capital raises. Many companies felt forced to announce equity rights issues, often pressured by lending banks. This was not a great episode in the listed real estate sector.

Most equity issues occurred in the UK, often in the form of rights issues, where more than £4.7 billion was raised in 2009 alone (see Table 8.1). High-profile investor Patrick Sumner, who published his diaries of this turbulent period for UK REITs in the *Financial Times* at the time, gave a good impression of what was going on: 'First of the majors out of the traps is Hammerson, whose message is clear: raise equity or be at a disadvantage in negotiations with banks and potential buyers of assets. Any breach means penal interest margins and a spiral into further trouble'.[2] There was a huge scramble for capital. Sumner in his diaries noted: 'There is a growing feeling that with £1.5 billion already raised, the door is closing'. The other UK majors followed suit, but not everything went smoothly, with SEGRO having to delay its rights issue by 24 hours 'because the UK Listing Authority, which has been aware of the timetable for a month, has been caught short and is not in a position to sign off'. Most of the capital calls were for balance sheet repair, although some companies, such as Helical Bar, GPE and SEGRO (in the case of its second equity issue to acquire Brixton), raised equity to purchase properties or portfolios opportunistically.

Having to repair balance sheets in the darkest of dark moments came at a high price: shares were issued at deep discounts – the issue price was on average more than 60% below the previous day's closing price – with high costs to be paid to investment banks/underwriters. Additionally, the deleveraging happened right at the bottom of the downturn, which, with hindsight, meant the companies reduced debt at the low point of the cycle when this should have happened at the high. Another issue was that most shareholders did not have enough capital to take up all their rights and had to sell them at a discount to others, who would make a fortune. On average, a sharp fall of around 12% in the shares was observed after the announcement of a rights issue, but a strong rebound of circa 40% occurred over the six months after the equity was issued.

76 REAL ESTATE RULES

Table 8.1 UK REITs equity issues, 2009

Company	Gross Proceeds	Balance Sheet	Opportunistic
Workspace Group	£87.0m	✓	
Helical Bar	£29.0m		✓
Hammerson	£609.0m	✓	
British Land	£767.0m	✓	
Landsec (formerly Land Securities)	£787.0m	✓	
SEGRO (formerly Slough Estates)	£524.0m	✓	
SEGRO (formerly Slough Estates)	£249.9m		✓
intu (formerly Liberty International)	£620.0m	✓	
intu (formerly Liberty International)	£280.5m	✓	
GPE (formerly Great Portland Estates)	£175.0m		✓
Shaftesbury	£158.0m	✓	
Grainger	£250.0m	✓	
Quintain Estates	£191.0m	✓	
Total	**£4,727.4m**		

Source: Company annual reports and press releases.

In Europe, there was much less equity issuance compared to the UK. While the UK property stocks would almost mirror their European peers one-on-one over 12 months before the rights issues, they would start to underperform severely over the following 12 months, resulting in circa 20% lower returns over the two-year period. While this is by no means academically proven, I do believe that the cost of the rights issues was in that order.

Brixton Bites the Dust

One UK company was late in taking deleveraging actions and did not make it: Brixton. The real estate investment trust (REIT) owned a portfolio of industrial and warehousing properties situated in prime UK locations with an emphasis on West London. Similar to the other UK REITs, the GFC hit them hard. Its CEO gained notoriety for including an image of the Four Horsemen of the Apocalypse on the front page of its 2008 interim report to capture the bleak atmosphere of the crisis, warning that the worst was yet to come. In the report, he also quoted lyric lines from Bob Dylan's 'All Along the Watchtower', ending with: 'None of them along the line know what any of it is worth'. The CEO finished his outlook statement by saying: 'Ultimately, the real "way out of here" will be when the economy, the financial world and the markets stabilise. However, in the near term, distress should bring opportunities and we are well placed to look to capitalise on these'.

I liked how the CEO spiced things up. He was clearly right that the situation was dire and that it was difficult to know the true value of property given that few transactions were taking place. However, he underestimated Brixton's financial situation. It was not 'well placed to capitalise' on opportunities; quite the opposite. It was close to breaching its debt covenants, had a high vacancy rate of 17.3% (and excluding developments of 10.6%) and carried a high liability for its derivative position. Brixton had successfully secured a waiver from its bank on a key covenant test until 31 July 2009, but after that, it could face an issue with its covenants.

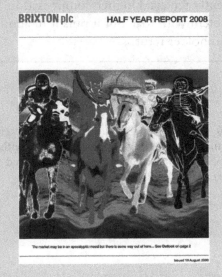

On 3 March 2009, the CEO was asked to stand down by the company board. Later, a major dispute became public with the CEO

(Continued)

(Continued)

threatened 'guerrilla war' against the board and hindered work on an emergency rights issue after his demand for a £1.88 million pension pay-out to retire was rejected. It was also said that he refused to cancel a 10-day ski holiday to Japan despite Brixton being 'on the brink of insolvency'. It was leaked that he told a fellow director, 'F★★★ that, I've paid for it'. Other colleagues did cancel their breaks. The case was later settled.

Brixton was in trouble, and competitor Slough Estates smelled its chance. In August 2009, it completed the purchase of Brixton at the bottom of the UK property cycle for £186.8 million (£1.1 billion enterprise value) financed through an opportunistic equity issue of £249.9 million (gross). The combination was renamed SEGRO. Brixton was no more. It failed, I believe, as a result of high financial leverage, management underestimating capital markets and not acting fast or rigorously enough, and misaligned incentives. Interestingly, despite Brixton being less than half the size of SEGRO, the CEO consistently received higher compensation. I do not necessarily have a problem with that, but it puts it in another light given the generated shareholder returns.

Notes

1. Citycon (2023) Press release, 9 June. https://www.citycon.com/newsroom/citycon-has-terminated-its-credit-rating-agreement-with-moodys-2023
2. Patrick Sumner (2009) 'Navigating some uncharted and hostile territory', *Financial Times*, 6 March.

Part III

Management

It is about strong management teams: value creation, skin in the game, consistency and transparency with the aim of building a track record and trust in capital markets. Without a track record or trust, there will be no capital available, or worse: it can lead to company failure.

Part III

Management

Chapter 9

Continuous Value Creation Is Key

Value Creation Leads to Superior Shareholder Value

It is often overlooked how important management is. But, in fact, there is a strong relationship between value creation by management and the share price. Economic value added (EVA) allows one to quantify whether a company is creating or destroying value. Simply put, companies should maximise returns from real estate, which is measured by the return on invested capital (ROIC), and minimise the cost from their liabilities, which is estimated by the weighted average cost of capital (WACC). Similar to the principal in Chapter 5, Soumen Das, CFO of SEGRO and formerly CFO of Capco, remarked: 'The best real estate people understand capital allocation and return on capital'.

The EVA is the difference between the ROIC and the WACC: value creation (destruction) is indicated by a positive (negative) spread. Evidence shows that a higher EVA spread has historically resulted in a higher shareholder return and a greater premium to net asset value (NAV). Figure 9.1 shows a strong relationship between forecast EVA and discount to NAV for a large sample of listed European property companies with a high R^2 of 77% (1% or 100% is perfect), which indicates that most stocks are fairly valued from a relative point of view (assuming my forecasts are correct). The lower the R^2, the more relative investment opportunities are available. Where the chart indicates that a company trades at a wider discount to NAV, but with a similar EVA spread, that company should be preferred versus its peer. Companies trading at a wide discount and with a highly negative EVA spread are value destroyers. They should only be bought if significant change is going to happen.

It all goes to show that value creation is key to performance. Yakir Gabay takes it one step further: 'Companies must make sure they have a great team, ideally with people working for you who are smarter than you'.

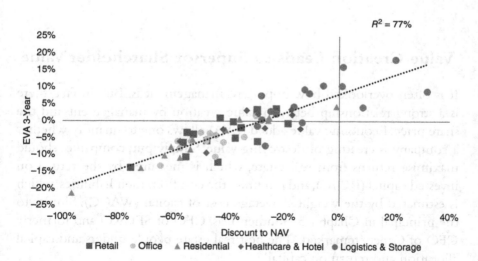

Figure 9.1 Strong relationship between EVA and discount to NAV
Source: Author estimates.

Optimising Total Returns from the Real Estate (ROIC)

In order to deliver superior returns from the assets, management needs to be continuously on the ball: focusing on continuous company optimisation and value addition. The best managers have a high degree of entrepreneurship, street smartness and the ability to think outside the box. For instance, Andrew Coombs is consistently proactive at Sirius. When they observed a significant spike in demand for storage during the COVID-19 pandemic, they strategically placed containers on their sites. And during the downturn in 2022/2023, they reached out to all owners of neighbouring properties to inquire whether they would be interested in selling. They managed to make some great acquisitions, adding significant value.

Examples of how real estate returns (ROIC) can be optimised:

- Portfolio sector/country/city allocation based on a long-term vision, i.e. focusing on real estate with the best risk/return prospects.
- Active management focused on revenue, capital expenditure (capex), costs and tax optimisation.
- Value add, e.g. extensions, refurbishments, developments, space management, platform creation, acquisitions/disposals, fund management for third parties.

The Perfect Negotiation – Anecdote by Jamie Ritblat

'A closing meeting of a deal usually took place at night (why people can't use the daytime, I will never know), with half a dozen issues to resolve and everyone eager to exchange but threatening to walk away if the deal wasn't done – the typical posturing. During my time at British Land, I accompanied Executive Vice-Chairman Cyril Metliss to close a deal. Upon arrival, we got straight into it, and Cyril essentially conducted a sermon, going through the list. He made one or two points, offered a compromise on another, and refused point blank to budge on the rest.

(Continued)

> *(Continued)*
>
> Before the others could even consider the offer, he stood up and asked if there was any supper. The legal team informed us that they had ordered some food, as was typical. Cyril shrugged and informed the other side that he and I were off for dinner at the local Italian around the corner, where he had booked a table. He assured them that we would be back in a while to give them time to consider his offer.
>
> We left the room and enjoyed dinner and a few bottles of wine. After an hour and a half, we returned to find the others still there, fed up with cold pizza and rubbish coffee, and essentially willing to agree to everything he had proposed. It was a master class in negotiation, closure, and the understanding of the human condition. I have often used the same routine with similar effect'.

Optimising the Capital Structure (WACC)

Significant value can be created or destroyed by getting the capital structure right or wrong. Companies that get it right 'sail' through downturns, benefit from someone else's misery and borrow on favourable terms, whilst those that get it wrong generate sub-optimal shareholder returns and frequently fight for survival when a real estate crisis hits.

Examples of how the WACC can be optimised:

- Note first of all that the actions on the assets (ROIC) can influence the risk profile of the company and hence the cost of capital. For example, properties in different sectors and locations have different risk and cash flow generation potential. Additionally, a company might have some lucrative developments, but developing tends to be a riskier business than managing a standalone asset.
- Amount of financial leverage.
- Timing of debt and equity issuance.
- Maturity profile of liabilities.
- Access to different financial products and sources of capital, including bond markets.
- Efficient tax structure.

- Trust, achieved by good corporate governance, e.g. accountability and transparency, and track record.
- Easy to understand business (model): the more complex, the higher the risk perceived by capital providers.

Cœur Défense – An Example of Strong Value Creation

Unibail's Key Office Development

The story of the office tower Cœur Défense has it all: the successful development of the largest office building in France, innovative financing, great market timing of its disposal and subsequently the largest distressed property sale due to the Great Financial Crisis (GFC). Cœur Défense is located in La Défense in the French capital, Paris. It was the key development project of the number one value creator among listed property companies at that time: Unibail (today URW). It comprised approximately 182,000 sq. m of (mainly) office space and 2,800 parking spaces. The architect was Jean-Paul Viguier. Unibail bought the land in 1998, after which it was

Source: Olivier Passalacqua/public domain/CC by S.A 2.5.

86 REAL ESTATE RULES

constructed by Bouygues in 32 months. It opened in May 2001. In 2001, the Cœur Défense conference centre was also acquired.

Successful Letting Process

By the end of 2000, Cœur Défense was 79% let, which would grow further to 94% in 2001. The occupier list was impressive: Crédit Lyonnais, AXA Investment Managers, Société Générale, ING, CCF-HSBC, PeopleSoft (the first six tenants to have signed up), Cap Gemini-Ernst & Young, Microsoft and SIFF-Energies (EDF Group). Most of them had a high credit quality rating of A or AA. All leases had nine-year terms, with some having a break clause after six years, leading to an average firm lease period of circa eight years. While the occupational market started to slow down in 2001 and subsequent years, as companies delayed decisions about taking on new space, Unibail continued to make letting progress, based on the location and quality of the building. An interesting fact: it mentioned in its annual report that the facades had been 'pressurised to enhance solar heat gain coefficient and minimise energy costs'. Something everyone is focused on today. By the end of 2002, 96% of Cœur Défense was let, resulting in a contracted rental income of €83.8 million and an estimated property valuation of €1,310 million. In 2004, the building was 99% occupied.

Innovative Financing

In December 2003, the Cœur Défense asset was refinanced through a securitisation of an €820 million mortgage loan (also called CMBS: commercial mortgage-backed security). The structure was similar to those backed by residential property in the US, which would later result in big problems during the GFC. There were four tranches, rated AAA, AA, A and BBB, each with 6.3 years maturity and a low weighted average margin of 67.5 basis points (bp) over the 3-month Euribor. It was arranged by Morgan Stanley, who placed it with 50 different investors. Based on a 2003 year-end valuation of €1,325 million for the building, the loan-to-value (LTV) ratio was approximately 62%, which was high. All in all, it was a great deal for Unibail, as it took advantage of favourable finance terms, whilst the loan was only recourse to the building, not the company. What is more, it would be the first step to a partial sale. In my view, this was important for Unibail, as the building was approximately 18% of its total portfolio at that time, there is generally a limited pool of potential buyers for (super) large assets, and it never hurts to lock in some money after a strong run. After all, real estate is cyclical and rather illiquid.

Partial Sale

In July 2004, Unibail was over the moon. I remember the management team running around bringing the good news to investors. It had significantly reduced its exposure to Cœur Défense, having sold 51% of the equity to Goldman Sachs' Whitehall Fund, retaining 49%. As the asset had risen further in value to €1,345 million (valued at a gross yield of approximately 6.8% excluding purchasers' costs) versus an initial capital expenditure for the project of €665 million, it also locked in a nice capital gain (+c.100%), and €686 million disposal proceeds were recorded. Unibail's total exposure was reduced to only €91 million: 49% of €30 million equity (€15 million) plus €76 million spread over three tranches: preferred equity, mezzanine and a senior loan. As the €820 million securitisation was now deconsolidated and €429 million of the subordinated debt was sold, Unibail's balance sheet debt was reduced by €1.25 billion. Its LTV fell from 40% to 28%. The company remained in charge of asset and property management of the building.

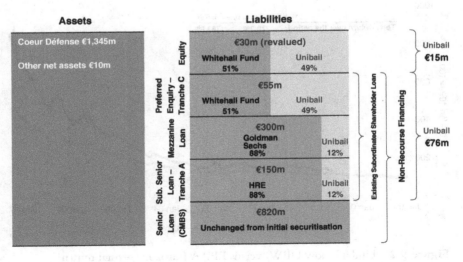

Source: Company; Author.

Significant Value Creation

Unibail had reduced its risk to the asset, but it would still heavily benefit from any increase or decline in value, as the asset itself was highly geared with an equity ratio of only 2.2% (or a multiplier of 45 times!). Real estate markets did go the right way. In fact, they were red hot, which resulted in a full sale of Cœur Défense for a whopping €2.11 billion, more than three times the initial development cost, on 27 March 2007 to Lehman Brothers Real Estate Partners. It was one of the largest deals in Europe for a single building at the time. The timing was great, as it would turn out to be right at the top.

The returns were mind-blowing. I estimate an internal rate of return (IRR) for Unibail of roughly between 30% and 40%, based on the (limited) data given in the annual reports. It should also be noted that the company only held 38% of the project at the beginning, while the fund Cross Roads Property Investors (managed by Unibail and in which it held 16% of the shares) had 40%, Bouygues 10% and Gothaer 12%. At the end of 1999, it bought out the fund, increasing its stake to 78%. In 2001, it purchased the other shares (by payment in Unibail shares), resulting in 100% ownership.

The deal made it possible for Unibail to pay out a special dividend of more than €1 billion to its shareholders in 2005. The disposal of Cœur Défense, balance sheet management and other lucrative deals were the big

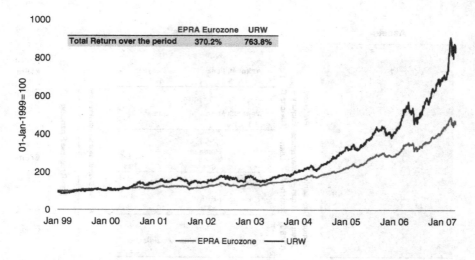

Figure 9.2 Unibail (now URW) versus EPRA Eurozone – total return
Source: FactSet.

Continuous Value Creation Is Key

drivers of its share price over the period 1 January 1999 to the end of March 2007: it generated a total return of 764% or an annualised return of approximately 30% versus the European Public Real Estate Association (EPRA) Eurozone benchmark index of 370% or an annualised return of approximately 21% (see Figure 9.2). Unibail had created strong value: its EVA spread was in double digits over 2004–2006, hitting +20% in 2006, which is extraordinary, as those spreads are normally between −3% and +3%.

While Unibail did a great job, Goldman Sachs did even better. I estimate that the Whitehall Fund saw its combined equity and preferred equity stake of €43.45 million gain about 900% in less than three years, resulting in an IRR of more than 130%! Its highly geared bet on the asset and the market had yielded a staggering performance.

Largest Distressed Sale

Whereas the story ended in 2007 for Unibail and Whitehall, the misery was only just beginning for Lehman. The GFC hit, resulting in falling property values and Lehman's bankruptcy in September 2008. In my view, two main issues arose related to the outstanding debt of €1.6 billion. First, Lehman Brothers was the hedging counterparty in the Cœur Défense transaction. It was impossible to find another counterparty to take over the position. Secondly, analysts estimated a much lower property value of between €1.1 and €1.6 billion for the building (I was at the lower end), meaning it would breach the 80% LTV covenant. I was quoted at that time in the press saying: 'We believe transaction prices may overshoot to the downside ... Buyers will be cherry picking'. As a result, safeguard protection was sought from creditors and a deadline received of July 2014 to pay back the debt.

Investors started to sniff around, trying to pick up the asset on the cheap. It was reported that Unibail was willing to purchase the asset back for €1.2–€1.3 billion. However, it was a special purpose vehicle controlled by Lone Star Real Estate Fund III that signed an agreement to purchase Cœur Défense for an estimated price of €1.3 billion in February 2014. At the time, the building was 76% occupied, with leases being short, having just 3.2 years to the first break and 5.3 years to expiry. In July 2017, Lone Star announced the signing of a binding agreement to sell Cœur Défense to Amundi Immobilier, Credit Agricole Assurances (two subsidiaries of the Credit Agricole banking group) and Primonial REIM for approximately €1.8 billion. The occupancy was around 95%. The asset was stabilised again.

M&A Can Add Value, but Frequently It Has Not

Everybody wants action and growth, but mergers and acquisitions (M&A) has too often been value destructive. Companies should not force it; it should make sense. Andrew Jones said: 'Company size is an outcome of a successful strategy'.

Potential Benefits of M&A

An acquirer can create value from M&A in different ways. It can expand into new markets, buy the target at an attractive price or extract value from the target that is not being realised by the current management, e.g. by optimising pricing and space, and improving its capital structure. In addition, the new combination could benefit from economies of scale: cost synergies, access to a wider range of capital (e.g. bond markets) and talent and increased liquidity of the shares.

But Be Careful with M&A

Unfortunately, M&A has not always created value for shareholders. Often, the purchase price was too high or the expected value-add was more limited than forecast. Additionally, significant problems have arisen with new combinations, such as excessive financial leverage, increased company complexity with too many business lines and entering unfamiliar markets. Remember, real estate is a local business, and local competitors often have the advantage in terms of culture, language, law, regulations, local habits, history and contacts. Moreover, the anticipated portfolio synergies often failed to materialise as communicated, or acquirers compromised on portfolio quality in favour of growth, which is not advisable. Finally, the resulting company sometimes became too large, acting more as a sector proxy, making it harder for management to add value. Toby Courtauld aptly summarised it: 'Be big enough to attract talent and capital, but small enough to move the needle and make a difference'.

Key mammoth mergers in the sector that drew significant attention, but not in a positive way, include Vonovia and Deutsche Wohnen, and Unibail-Rodamco and Westfield.

Vonovia: One Bridge Too Far

Deutsche Annington's ambition was to become the industry consolidator. It went on an acquisition spree (see Table 9.1) starting with GAG-FAH in 2015, after which the combination was called Vonovia. At the end of 2021, it would absorb its industry rival Deutsche Wohnen on the third attempt, becoming the industry mogul with a portfolio worth more than €90 billion, consisting of approximately 565,000 units, mainly situated in Germany. Deutsche Wohnen had previously acquired GSW in 2013. To finance the acquisition, Vonovia executed a mega rights issue of €8.1 billion, which was approximately 4% of the total market capitalisation of the stocks included in the real estate benchmark index EPRA Europe.

Table 9.1 Vonovia: Major acquisitions

Acquisitions	Announcement Date	Completion Date
GAGFAH	01–Dec–14	06–Mar–15
Südewo	14–Jun–15	08–Jul–15
Conwert Immobilien	05–Sep–16	10–Jan–17
BUWOG	18–Dec–17	26–Mar–18
Victoria Park	03–May–18	28–Jun–18
Hembla	23–Sep–19	07–Nov–19
Bien Ries	05–Mar–20	02–Apr–20
Deutsche Wohnen	24–May–21	27–Oct–21

Source: Vonovia annual reports and press releases.

Although there were merits for the acquisition-led strategy initially, such as economies of scale, share liquidity and access to bond markets, I believe Vonovia became too big after the Deutsche Wohnen transaction, particularly relative to its European counterparts. Not only were additional synergies limited at this point, but Vonovia was also now more of a proxy for the German residential market. Incremental value added would only have a limited impact on the overall result. Furthermore, its enormous size put it more in the public eye, particularly of politicians. Vonovia had to watch its steps more carefully.

Additionally, there were capital markets implications. Its market capitalisation rose to more than €40 billion, which meant two things. First of all, the company was now too large for the capital available from dedicated real estate investors and, as such, it turned its attention more to large general equity investors and hedge funds, who are more fickle. If there is better value elsewhere or the theme is against real estate, they are gone or go short the stock, i.e. bet on the downside. This is exactly what happened in 2022. Secondly, Vonovia was now more than 10% of the benchmark index (at certain points even close to 16%), which was problematic because many property funds could not invest more than 10% of their fund in one holding.

All of this could have been manageable if the company 'wrapper', i.e. how the real estate was managed and financed, was in order. Now that the company had become a mega tanker, it should have been run efficiently and with a bullet-proof balance sheet. While the former was true, Vonovia got caught out on the latter. The ratio of net debt to recurring EBITDA was more than 17 times by my estimates. When market sentiment started to change for the worse, the question increasingly arose: who was going to lend the company billions as its debt matured? This issue could not be easily solved by portfolio sales because transactions were drying up in the tough market environment, and the company would need to dispose of significant amounts to make an impact on its asset base of approximately €90 billion. Soon financial markets began to price in the chance of a significant, highly discounted equity issue, further pushing its share price down. Vonovia had become a risk for the whole sector, as its precarious balance sheet was affecting market sentiment in general. For me, it was one of the biggest sector risks at that time.

The Deutsche Wohnen takeover was a bridge too far. Vonovia's share price fell back all the way to its initial public offering (IPO) price almost 10 years ago (Figure 9.3). The 'Castles Made of Sand' were washed away by tightening monetary policy, exacerbated by taking on too much debt in the past. Vonovia frantically tried to sell assets, but facing difficulty, it resorted to creative disposal structures. In these structures, buyers took a stake in portfolios but received a larger share of the income. However, it did avoid a highly discounted (rescue) rights issue.

Figure 9.3 Vonovia – share price back at IPO price
Source: Adapted from FactSet.

The Unibail-Rodamco-Westfield Saga

What was remarkable about Vonovia's misstep is that Unibail-Rodamco[1] made a similar mistake three years earlier, which should have been a lesson for the industry. In June 2018 (having announced the deal at the end of 2017), Unibail-Rodamco, at that time the leading shopping mall player in Europe, completed the acquisition of Westfield, which owned and operated 35 shopping centres in the US and the UK, to create Unibail-Rodamco-Westfield (URW) with a total asset base of €62 billion (of which €18.4 billion came from Westfield). URW had expanded its empire from Europe to include the UK and US.

The price paid for Westfield looked full, with a net rental income yield of approximately 4%, especially as not all its shopping centres were of top quality and its US peers were trading at sizeable discounts to NAV, implying rental yields of around 6%. While there was some rationale for creating a high-quality shopping centre platform in multiple countries, and the overall quality of URW's portfolio increased because of the transaction, retail trends were clearly weak in the UK and US. Furthermore, financial leverage increased and it was unclear how significant top-line synergies would be realised between the US and European portfolios. URW was aware that action was needed. It was targeting €100 million of synergies over five years, of which €99 million were already achieved by December 2019, and €3 billion of disposals to de-gear the balance sheet.

However, Green Street calculated that URW's LTV ratio was now 47% on their estimates and the net debt-to-EBITDA ratio was 11.4×. To have a similar balance sheet as the US-listed real estate investment trust (REIT) Simon Property Group, i.e. an LTV ratio of around 30% and net debt-to-EBITDA of 6–6.5×, it would require €3 billion of fresh equity on top of asset disposals of approximately €12 billion. Much more action would be needed than the communicated €3 billion sales target. One could argue that the US is not Europe, but the fact remains that leverage was on the high side.

I was not overly enthusiastic at the time. The price paid was too high, and I did not really buy into the rationale of 'going global'. I did not believe that there was much to be gained from bringing retailers to other countries, because retailers want to be in the best malls for them anyway. Besides, 'going global' often comes at a cost, as real estate is a local business and historically cross-border transactions have destroyed more value than they created. Moreover, URW's investor community was local, and most of them (including me) had little familiarity with the US portfolio, which accounted for 22% of the enlarged entity. If investors do not know something or have doubts, they price in a discount. Nevertheless, almost 95% of Unibail-Rodamco shareholders approved the transaction.

Then COVID hit in 2020, which brought the URW empire to its knees, particularly because of its high financial leverage. Credit rating agencies S&P and Moody's started to downgrade its debt. Short sellers piled in. The URW shares were absolutely hammered, returning −83% from the beginning of the year until their low point on 29 September 2020 and −74% since the announcement of the Westfield acquisition in December 2017 (Figure 9.4).

On 16 September 2020, URW communicated its RESET plan, a strategy to deleverage by more than €9 billion. The plan included a fully underwritten €3.5 billion rights issue, reducing cash dividends by €1 billion over the next two years, a further €800 million reduction in development and non-essential operating capex, and €4 billion of disposals by year-end 2021. URW believed this was the right action to take: issuing equity to secure necessary access to capital markets by protecting its strong investment grade rating, especially given its high amount of (gross) debt of €27.4 billion and high dependency on bond markets. Whilst management was, of course, not pleased to have to raise equity, it was concerned that the company would not be able to maintain a sufficiently strong credit rating to finance its debt maturities. Furthermore, it believed that the bond market was effectively closed during COVID and that banks could not be relied upon to fill a potential funding gap.

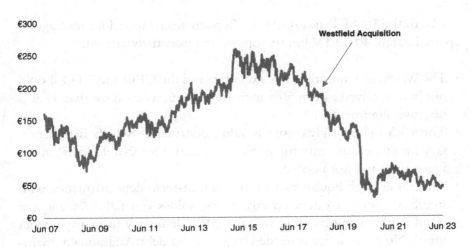

Figure 9.4 URW share price
Source: Data from Factset.

But on 15 October 2020, a frontal activist campaign was launched against management's plan. Its slogan: REFOCUS NOT RESET. The masterminds behind this plan were significant: former Unibail Chairman and CEO Léon Bressler (through real estate private equity firm Aermont, which he co-owned) and technology and telecommunications entrepreneur billionaire Xavier Niel (through his vehicle Rock Investment). Bressler, who was at the helm at Unibail for 14 years until 2006, had one of the best reputations in the industry, while Niel is best known for founding Iliad, a French internet service provider and mobile operator. Forbes estimated Niel's net worth at $8.2 billion in August 2022. Together they controlled 4.1% of URW shares through their vehicles. Niel's ownership would grow to 4.4% by year-end 2020, later increasing further to 14.6% by the end of 2021 and 25.51% (for the Niel family) as of 10 October 2024.[2]

The activists went all in, being highly critical of URW's management and board, presenting an alternative plan and launching a media campaign that included a website (refocusnotreset.com) and presence in the press. Additionally, another former Unibail Chairman and CEO (2006–2013), Guillaume Poitrinal, joined in, calling the RESET plan 'null and void'. It was clear that the former Unibail leadership was extremely upset with URW's value destruction over the years.

Both the RESET and REFOCUS plans aimed to reduce leverage to approximately 40% LTV, but the opposition essentially argued:

- The Westfield acquisition was a disaster (and the CEO and CFO should not have received a circa 50% increase in remuneration for that. That is negative alignment!).
- The €3.5 billion rights issue is value destructive: 'which is unnecessary, misguided and extremely value destructive for shareholders', at the worst time and not needed.
- There is enough liquidity to cover medium-term debt maturities, with significant room to debt covenants, e.g. values can fall 30%, and the bond market is functioning well for URW (contrary to management's view). No new equity is needed to pay down debt. Additionally, maintaining the A- credit rating should not be a goal in itself.
- The US assets, excluding the UK, including offices and convention centres, should be sold (when the time is right).
- Three Supervisory Board members should be added to strengthen the board: Bressler, Niel and a third independent member (Susana Gallardo).

Interestingly, the pillars of the activist campaign were the work of the CFO and Deputy CFO (the cash and credit lines available plus terms on the debt) and a supportive European Central Bank at the time, which was purchasing bonds, including those of listed real estate companies. However, the URW management and board judged that this was not enough, arguing: 'Addressing the capital structure issue with a hypothetical sale of the US portfolio in 2–3 years is reckless … and may force asset sales or a larger capital raise with less favourable terms down the road … [The RESET plan will] safeguard against a potential negative financial spiral… Act now rather than later'.[3]

Both parties started to lobby for their plans, with URW needing two-thirds approval for the rights issue. But then property stocks, especially retail-related, started to rally from 6 November on the back of a potential vaccine for COVID-19. I believe this influenced the vote and might even have been the deciding factor. The rights issue was narrowly voted down on 10 November 2020 (with approximately 62% in favour but about 5% below the threshold). In addition, the three proposed board members, including the two activists, were voted onto the board with around 60% of the vote. URW's management and supervisory board had lost.

The activists won and took swift action. On 13 November 2020, several board changes were made with Bressler becoming Chairman. On 18 November, a new CEO (Jean-Marie Tritant) was announced, followed later by a new CFO (Fabrice Mouchel).

It is true that credit agencies downgraded URW's debt and that URW was still deleveraging in 2023, but the company kept its investment grade (S&P BBB+ in May 2023) despite a continued difficult climate in 2022–2023. Overall, I believe it was right that the rights issue was cancelled. I agreed that the bond market would remain open. Besides, the cost of the new equity issue at that time would be too high. As said before, it is often argued that it does not matter when rights issues are executed, as every shareholder gets an equal (pro rata) right to participate. But this does not hold up in times of trouble when there is a shortage of capital and the issue price is extremely low. Shareholders had clearly shown their discontent.

Notes

1. Unibail merged with Rodamco Europe in 2007, although in reality it was more a takeover by Unibail.
2. French Autorité des marchés financiers (AMF), www.amf-france.org
3. URW (2020) 'Reset is the right plan for URW', 19 October. https://cdn.urw.com/-/media/Corporate~o~Sites/Unibail-Rodamco-Corporate/Files/Homepage/INVESTORS/Reset-Plan/20201019-RESET-is-the-right-plan-for-URW_onlyEN.pdf?revision=459e338e-33d4-45d6-a2e7-a61cac62ac4d

Chapter 10

Radical Action Needed in Case of Shareholder Value Destruction

Indeed, companies should strive to benefit all stakeholders, but it is quite simple: if, ultimately, there's no track record of creating shareholder value, there won't be capital available for future growth. This results in the company becoming stagnant, trading at a discounted valuation. Remember: real estate companies are primarily investment vehicles. The only way to change this situation is for management to operate at maximum efficiency. The longer this doesn't happen, the more dissatisfied the capital markets become, exacerbating the problem and making it harder to resolve. Eventually, investors may lose interest altogether, necessitating radical action.

Change Management, Board and/or Governance

It may sound harsh, but it is often in everyone's interest: if the CEO (or a certain manager or board member) does not perform, he or she should be replaced as soon as possible. The sooner, the better. I've learned this over the years. Don't let it drag on, as it will only make things exponentially worse. Shareholders, and especially boards, have a crucial role in this, but boards are often too slow to act, while shareholders often just sell their shares and move on. Beware of complacent boards or boards filled with people who only care about whether the company meets legal and stock listing requirements, without a real passion for the business.

For instance, there was a highly successful CEO of a European shopping centre REIT who founded the company and built it up with a strong management team. The company thrived, but after about 20 years, the CEO began to lose his touch. I recall one conference where he dismissed the impact of the internet on shopping centres entirely. He seemed increasingly out of step, and confidence in the market started to wane. The board did not intervene, possibly because most members were puppets of the CEO. Eventually, the CEO departed, but it was too late and under less-than-ideal circumstances. It's regrettable, as he had truly achieved remarkable things, but he stayed on beyond the right time to leave.

Return of Capital

If a high valuation discount persists, companies should consider alternative ways to create value, such as a share or debt buyback, a special dividend or even putting the company up for sale, as successfully done by many companies, including Green REIT and St Modwen. Doing nothing is not an option: management's reputation will be tarnished, capital markets will lose faith in the company and it will, of course, hinder the growth of the listed sector, as the financial community begins to associate property companies with long-term underperforming businesses.

A special comment on share buybacks: if the balance sheet is secure, the portfolio is in good condition and management is strong, a buyback could be a good plan. If not, problems are likely to worsen, particularly as many management teams are often late in recognising a market downturn – frequently the reason why the stock trades at a significant discount.

Before the Global Financial Crisis (GFC), many companies embarked on share buybacks, only to issue equity at deeply discounted prices a couple of years later. Other companies managed to get it wrong even in shorter time frames. The Dutch real estate company NSI, for instance, bought back shares in January 2012 at €8.74, only to place shares at €8.30 three months later in April. Buy high, sell low equals value destruction. Fortunately, there are also companies that got it right, such as UK REIT GPE, which raised £304 million of capital in total in 2009 and 2012, only to return £616 million of capital over the period 2017–2020.

Circle Property Trust went as far as to liquidate itself, as it remained significantly undervalued and uninvestible on the stock market. A wise decision for all involved.

Circle Property Trust: Liquidating Itself

Circle Property was a specialist property investor focusing on regional offices in the UK, i.e. cities like Birmingham. Since 2002, the company built a track record. For example, it acquired an 80,000 sq. ft. office in the centre of Bristol for just over £4 million after the GFC and later sold it in 2022 for £20 million. I learnt about Circle Property at the start of 2016, when John Arnold (CEO) and Edward Olins (COO) came to our office to market their initial public offering (IPO). At that time, its portfolio comprised 16 assets valued at about £74 million. I liked the management and what they did. However, the company was too small for us and its expected share trading not significant. We could not risk being stuck in an illiquid company. Many other investors echoed this. Nevertheless, Circle Property went ahead and listed on AIM in February 2016 with a small market capitalisation of £42 million and little new money being raised.

The stock continuously traded at a significant valuation discount, despite management's best efforts, including ongoing transparent communication with the market, value creation achievements and outperformance compared to the wider market. The company was tiny, which not only meant it had a relatively high cost base, but also that it would take approximately 1,000 days to buy a £5 million stake, assuming one bought 25% of the volume of shares traded every day; it is hard to buy more to avoid influencing the share price (unless large blocks become available). The stock was uninvestable for institutional investors.

Figure 10.1 Circle Property – total return, 2016–2023
Source: FactSet.

Realising that the company was unable to grow and perhaps concluding it should never have IPO'd in the first place, Circle started to look at alternative ways to move forward, including mergers and acquisitions (M&A). On 14 February 2022, the company communicated that it would be liquidated in the next two to three years, debt paid down and capital returned to shareholders. From the IPO up until that date, Circle had generated a total return of 83.2%, outperforming its UK peers by 51.1%. An incentive package was introduced for management to ensure optimal execution for all parties involved: the directors would each be eligible to receive a cash incentive payment worth up to £2.5 million each, based on exit prices achieved. On 4 May 2023, Circle announced it had sold its last property. Its stock listing was cancelled on 1 June 2023. Its shares had returned 78%, or an annualised 8.3%, since its IPO, versus the UK real estate benchmark European Public Real Estate Association (EPRA) return of −4%, or an annualised −0.4% (Figure 10.1). It is a pity the company did not make it, but it was too small in the first place. At least the Circle story ended relatively well for all parties involved. Everyone could move on with their heads held high.

Chapter 11

Overconfidence Leads to Downfall

It is great to have management with conviction, but if it becomes 'cocky' or results in an unlimited bull story (overconfidence), one needs to think twice. When the European real estate markets were in a 'boom' phase up to the first part of 2007, some CEOs started to exhibit invincible behaviour. Not a good omen of what was to come! Philip Charls, former CEO of European Public Real Estate Association (EPRA), notes: 'When people became cocky, it often went from up to down. The introduction of a Hubris Index would help investors to better monitor CEO's suffering from this syndrome'. Or, as per Michiel te Paske: 'You have to be careful when people believe their own hype. They start to confuse their personal brilliance with their market performance'.

Capital & Regional – The Remarkable Example of Overconfidence

A remarkable example of overconfidence is Capital & Regional (C&R). They just believed the bull run would continue indefinitely. From its 2006 annual report:

> We believe the long-term fundamentals for UK retail and leisure remain strong. A growing population with a high propensity to spend is serviced by a restricted supply of retail space, which remains well below other developed economies, particularly the US. In these circumstances, long-term rental growth can be expected. There have been some concerns that retail investment yields have fallen too far. We do not agree.

That turned out to be wrong. The net property yields for their UK exposure were low, particularly as transfer duties were not taken into account: Mall fund (shopping centres) yield was 4.6%, Junction (retail parks) 3.29% and X-Leisure 4.86%. Reportedly, they even dismissed potential bidders for the company. However, their biggest mistake was having financial leverage that was too high, with a loan-to-value (LTV) ratio of 56%. That was 'gambling' with the company. Additionally, they should never have boasted about their performance in the way they did in their 2006 annual report (see Figures 11.1 and 11.2).

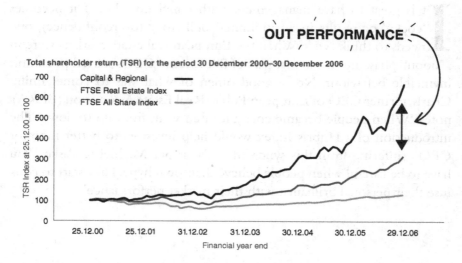

Figure 11.1 Capital & Regional – total shareholder return, 2000–2006
Source: Capital & Regional annual report, 2006.

Overconfidence Leads to Downfall

Track record

	NAV growth	NAV per share	Dividend per share	Dividend growth
December 1996		223p + 19%	3.0p + 20%	
December 1997	19% pa	272p + 22%	3.5p + 17%	24% pa
December 1998		321p + 18%	4.25p + 21%	
December 1999		370p + 17%	5.0p + 18%	
December 2000		350p −5%	5.5p + 10%	
December 2001		336p −4%	6.0p + 11%	
December 2002	34% pa	392p + 17%	7.0p + 17%	42% pa
December 2003		521p + 33%	9.0p + 29%	
December 2004		710p + 36%	14.0p + 56%	
December 2005		985p* + 38%	18.0p + 40%	
December 2006		1272p* + 29%	26.0p + 44%	

WOW (again)!

Figure 11.2 Capital & Regional's track record
Source: Capital & Regional annual report, 2006.

Its performance was indeed amazing. The C&R shares returned 674% from 25 December 2000 until the peak of the market. However, the stock crashed completely once the downturn hit, falling by 96% and remaining in the doldrums for a long time. The new management faced an uphill battle to ensure the company's survival. When later asked if the fire at its Walthamstow mall in London marked the lowest point, they responded that it did not even rank among the top ten challenges – underscoring the difficulties of the period. If we update the outperformance chart from the

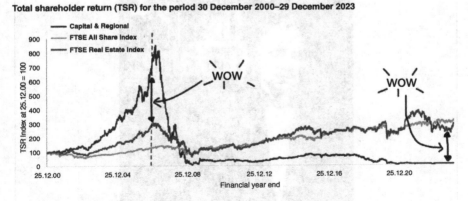

Figure 11.3 Capital & Regional – total shareholder return, 2000–2023
Source: Author based on Capital & Regional's 2006 annual report and FactSet data for subsequent years.

annual report to today, it shows that the report almost exactly marked the height of the boom, after which the outperformance turned into massive underperformance (see Figure 11.3): pride goes before a fall.

Der Deal Macher

A well-regarded analyst was critical of a German property company because the business did not produce any cash flow or cash earnings, despite its high leverage, as its entire profits were made up of revaluation gains on trading assets. When he visited them, he saw a Godfather-style movie poster in the office, but instead of Marlon Brando and the title 'The Godfather', it had a picture of the CEO and 'Der Dealmacher'. The CFO greeted him in front of an investor with: 'Ah, hello, the black sheep amongst our analysts!' From my experience, you tend to be right if management teams call you names like that. In this case, it was no different. Soon the company would be fighting for survival (2008/2009) and would not make it. The same analyst was blocked by another German company due to his critical stance. The story goes that they organised an investor boat trip, intentionally selecting a boat with a low ceiling so that the rather tall analyst had to bend over throughout the entire trip.

Source: 7th Street Theatre Hoquiam/Flickr.com.

Chapter 12

Corporate Governance Should Be Top Nudge

Good corporate governance is paramount for a well-functioning company. The aim is to create trust between management, the board and the stakeholders, which is key to creating value over time. Poor governance results in long-term underperformance and can literally destroy a company. Checks and balances need to be in place. Companies should be clean, transparent and aligned with shareholders' interests.

In the past, the public real estate sector lacked transparency and was dominated by 'cowboys' who treated the business as their personal lifestyle company. Fortunately, the sector has significantly improved over the years. Enhanced stock exchange rules, new legislation, the introduction of real estate investment trust (REIT) structures globally and the establishment of European Public Real Estate Association (EPRA), the industry body for listed real estate in Europe, have all contributed to substantial advancements in transparency, consistency, accountability and alignment within the

108

European property sector. Alan Carter, one of the industry's icon analysts, remarked: 'There is no comparison with the past: back then, companies were run for management's benefit rather than for shareholders. It was often unclear which properties the company owned. Full-year results took a long time to publish and included only limited information, such as earnings per share (EPS), net asset value (NAV), dividend per share, and pre-tax profit. Today, there is much more information available'. But it was not just the real estate industry that became more professional; the financial world did too. My experiences at the Amsterdam Exchanges (AEX) illustrate how financial markets have evolved over time: see the next box 'Those Were the Days'.

Those Were the Days – Professionalism Sets In

I spent time in various departments of the Amsterdam Exchanges (AEX) in 1998–2000. It was fascinating, especially my time at Market Surveillance on the Option Exchange, which was still 'open outcry', i.e. a face-to-face auction where hundreds of people physically traded with each other. It was a bit of a wild west. This was a world of 'cowboys' wearing coloured jackets who could crunch numbers very quickly and make lots of money. Not everyone was as intrigued by the Exchanges as I was. From time to time, protestors would sneak in, unfolding banners from the balustrade above the trading floor. When that happened, a group of big guys from the Exchanges would be assembled to push them out as quickly as possible. That was how it was done in those days.

But things were not perfect. For example, I had to develop a valuation system because some market participants changed bid-ask quotes (the prices at which they would buy (bid) or sell (ask)) at the end of the day to influence the valuation of their positions (and therefore how much they could borrow). There were other problems, such as drug usage, which left clear traces in the toilets at the end of the day. Drug use was very high amongst market makers. Then there was the behaviour. I remember a guy who arrived by car but had not reserved a parking spot. The kind reception lady told him he could not enter the garage, upon which he cursed heavily,

Corporate Governance Should Be Top Nudge 109

asking who the hell she was and declaring that he had lots of money. There was also the phenomenon of 'farthing in the crowd'. Yes, you read that correctly. If you were guilty of that, you would be fined 1,000 guilders (c. €450). Or the issue of trading other goods outside trading hours, such as expensive watches.

However, this fascinating open outcry system was gradually coming to its end. Perhaps the most telling sign was the appearance of market makers from the US with handhelds (little computers) in the crowd, competing for business with locals who were doing the numbers in their heads. Clearly, this development was not what the locals wanted. Each time a floor broker came up with a trade to be executed, a local market maker (they would take turns) would push the American or distract him in another way so that he could not use his handheld and win the business. But it could not stop the imminent end of 'open outcry' and the move to computers, which eventually happened after almost 400 years on 6 December 2002.

Risk Management

In the first decade of this century, a property company had an IT department that also operated its own IT business. This clearly should not have been the case. Risk management ensures that processes are in place to control risk and eliminate fraud, such as procedures for employees regarding the renting, buying and selling of properties. For example, I am aware of a past instance where a potential buyer of company assets gave a free scooter to an employee in return for a lower price for the asset. Guidelines for real estate valuations, which should be carried out by external valuers without any pressure from the company for a particular result, are also important.

In addition, risk management encompasses information and communications technology (cybersecurity), treasury (hedging and spreading of risk), liquidity (ensuring sufficient cash flow at all times), taxes (optimising taxes in a clean manner without 'dodgy' structures), developments (cost management and timing), environmental, social and governance (adherence to regulations regarding energy and carbon reduction), human resources (employee procedures) and debtors (ensuring they will pay), among other aspects.

Transparency

The industry needs consistent, concise data in line with industry guidelines and specific to its business, avoiding vague language. For example, some companies always report to the market positively, sometimes even omitting crucial data or altering the calculation of certain parameters. It can also happen that a company reports perfectly within the requirements or codes, but certain details should have been disclosed based on common sense.

The emphasis should be on transparency, not manipulation. It is important for companies to communicate consistently 'in the same language' both externally and internally, i.e. using the same definitions, to avoid making poor decisions. The first thing we did when we started ICAMAP was to circulate a glossary of real estate terms so that everyone was clear about the type of yield or NAV being discussed.

Governance Dynamics

Some companies have become too bureaucratic, leading to stagnation and unnecessary complexity. For a company to be successful, there should be an optimal balance between checks and balances on one side and entrepreneurial spirit on the other. As Alec Pelmore, together with Robert Fowlds, one of the former star analysts at Merrill Lynch (now Bank of America), says:

> 'How is the relationship between the CEO, the team, the board, and shareholders? How are the dynamics? How are decisions being made? Is the information given to the board selective? The big question is what input the executive really wants from the board? In many cases, it is just the formality of the agreement'.

In my view, there needs to be some kind of chemistry between the CEO and the board, and between the chairperson and the CEO. Too much bureaucracy or a lack of trust can paralyse the company or result in mishaps. Pelmore continues:

> Often, the CEO does not have an influence on appointments to the board. In many cases, he or she does not really relate to or trust them. The CEO does not go to the board with a problem unless he has the solution. So, if he has a real problem, where does he go? Does he get on

Corporate Governance Should Be Top Nudge

well enough with the Chairman or CFO? Not always. He cannot trust investment bankers, who give advice most likely to bring them fees. One CEO told me he turns to his father for good impartial advice! Another always went to his ex-boss.

To ensure the right chemistry, the composition, variety of disciplines and quality of the non-executive board (in a way they are cost-effective advisors to management) are all crucial elements. The current push for diversity on the board is a positive for the real estate sector, which tends to be male dominated. However, it is important to strike a balance and avoid swinging too far in the other direction, pre-emptively excluding individuals who can make valuable contributions.

Remuneration

Most investors have no issue with management being well compensated if they deliver, i.e. if they hit their targets and create significant shareholder returns. However, if performance has been lacklustre and the compensation high, that is obviously asking for trouble.

Allergic to Spiralling Salaries

I am hugely allergic to boards, advised by external consultants, who raise the salaries of executives simply because the company has grown and, therefore, the compensation packages are now considered 'low' compared to management teams at similarly sized or larger companies, even in different industries! To me, this just leads to an upward spiral in salaries and an incentive to grow, but over the years I have not always seen a clear relationship to total shareholder return – quite the contrary! Personally, I do not understand these super high salaries: I prefer a sensible salary (good enough to live on) with pay linked to performance.

Within the listed real estate industry, Unibail-Rodamco-Westfield (URW) significantly increased the compensation packages of its CEO and CFO in 2018 after it took over Westfield. The deal was indeed life changing for the company, but unfortunately in a negative way. In 2021, remuneration was drastically reduced for the new management (see Figure 12.1).

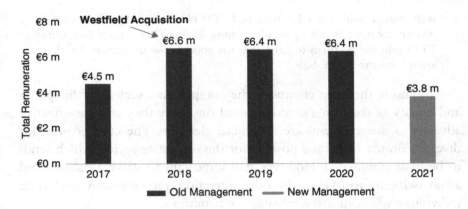

Figure 12.1 URW – jump in total remuneration paid or granted (CEO and CFO) after mergers and acquisitions (M&A)
Source: Company annual report, 2021.

Gaming

The alignment between management and investors is essential, as investors need to be sure that management creates value, not just for itself. The problem is that performance measures can be 'gamed', i.e. management can influence the measures in a favourable direction to earn a significant bonus, but this can come at the expense of other variables, which may move negatively, resulting in shareholder value destruction.

Examples of gaming performance measures:

> **EPS:** When I studied the incentive programmes of Dutch real estate companies at the end of the 1990s, I found that in every case where growth in EPS, or something similar, was introduced in the compensation package, the measure significantly rose in the following years. Great result? Not quite. It destroyed future shareholder returns, as it incentivised management to increase financial leverage, use cheaper short-term debt, buy higher-yielding lower-quality properties and employ accounting tricks. As a result, the companies were not well positioned when the next downturn hit, resulting in significant shareholder value destruction.
>
> **Reward per project:** A UK development company rewarded its executive a bonus per successful development project. Some projects were great, others were not. The result was that the executive

received a high bonus for the winners, but the total shareholder return was poor, as shareholders also absorbed the cost of the losers.

NAV: At some other companies, management was rewarded based on NAV, resulting in inflated property valuations. There have been instances where management ran the company into the ground, as cash flow was seen as less important, e.g. by keeping buildings vacant in hopes of securing higher rents.

Acquisition bonus: A German company rewarded management for acquisitions, but not necessarily for purchases made at attractive prices or prospects for shareholders.

Adjusted funds from operations (AFFO): This is a cash earnings measure, but it deducts capital expenditure (capex). It is very easy to simply reduce capex in a year to achieve a higher AFFO, but this has no link to shareholder value.

Total shareholder return (TSR): There are many examples here as well. It can lead to misplaced optimism and selective reporting, aiming to push the share price higher, but not justified by the actual earnings development.

As a result, performance measures cannot be used in isolation. They should be well defined and bulletproof under different scenarios. In addition, investors should carefully study performance measures and assess how they have changed compared to the previous year. This often provides clues about management's future actions. For example, if the dividend is suddenly excluded, it might signal an upcoming dividend cut or indicate that modest growth is expected.

Shareholder Alignment

Management compensation packages should consist of a salary, annual bonus and long-term incentive plan. TSR should be the overriding element, but it should be combined with carefully selected performance measures that cannot be gamed. In my view, to achieve optimal alignment between executives and shareholders, the following ingredients are important: a scorecard, a long-term incentive plan focused on TSR, investment by the executives in shares and common sense by the board. We are looking for alignment, simplicity and transparency.

Annual bonus based on a scorecard: To mitigate 'gaming', I prefer a scorecard for a short-term bonus with a number of performance measures focused on operational performance (e.g. like-for-like vacancy, like-for-like rental growth, costs), balance sheet (e.g. level of leverage, maturity profile, access to bond markets, shareholder interaction), portfolio (e.g. level of capex, disposals, acquisitions, delivery of developments, level of carbon emissions) and other more personal goals. Depending on the company's strategic goals, the scorecard can focus on a maximum of eight to ten measures with different weightings of importance, but measures that are hard to quantify should not be more than a third. Different managers can have different weightings for measures focused on their area of expertise, although there should be a common measure included in all scorecards, e.g. recurring profit.

Long-term incentive plan focused on TSR: This involves payment for share performance in shares with a lock-in period of a minimum of three years. It should be both relative and absolute, e.g. underperformance versus peers results in no payment, and higher returns correspond to a higher bonus.

Skin in the game: Boards should ensure that management has enough skin in the game, not by giving them the shares for free, but by making them genuinely 'feel' they bought the shares with hard-earned money. This will reduce the risk of management making irrational decisions. A top executive's stake should be worth at least three to five times their salary. If the executive does not have that amount of money, they would need to invest their annual bonus in shares until the threshold is reached. Equally, clawback policies should be in place to recapture payments in the event of misstatements or breaches of contract.

Common sense: The board should use common sense by setting the level of salaries and evaluating the scorecard, as unforeseen events may occur or the link between management performance and shareholder value creation may ultimately be weak. Unfortunately, this is often missing, with boards hiding behind rigid rules or being afraid to make decisions that have to be explained and/or defended at annual general meetings (AGMs). In addition, boards should dedicate sufficient time to comprehensively understand the business and set realistic targets. Too often, they are influenced by management, who naturally prefer easier targets.

Compounding Goodwill

Although shareholder value creation is the ultimate goal, the way to achieve this is to think of, work with, understand and help all stakeholders. This does not mean spending excessive amounts on unrelated projects to look good with shareholders' money, but rather showing genuine involvement in stakeholders' interests to help them move forward. This approach will build goodwill and pay off over time.

Yakir Gabay states: 'Maintain lasting and close relationships with partners, tenants, bankers, analysts, brokers, investors, credit rating agencies, traders, and the like across multiple organisations and sectors. Eventually, success in business comes from both good numbers, but even more important is the long-term relationships one creates in their career'.

Part IV

Investing in Listed Real Estate

Investing in listed real estate vehicles is about identifying future trends and finding the hidden 'pearls', i.e. those that are attractively priced under different economic scenarios.

Part IV

Investing in Listed Real Estate

Chapter 13

Scrutinise Property Investment Vehicles

First Impressions Can Be Misleading

The real estate sector is full of people with great stories and investment advice, often tilted to the positive side for too long. Companies frequently boast about having the 'prettiest child in the playground', and the press captures attention with sensational headlines. However, reality is frequently more nuanced or even the opposite. It is paramount to conduct detailed analysis: this reduces the chance of poor investment decisions and increases the probability of finding the highly profitable, unloved trade.

Examples of misleading situations (that happened):

Positive company reporting whilst its situation is dire: A company put the screaming title 'Best operating results in Group's history' above its 2023 results, but in fact, it was struggling with a debt pile on its balance sheet.

Disposals above book value: The assets were reduced in value before the sale and/or included debt or other sweeteners at advantageous terms. Similarly, a company announced a profitable development, but it had to take a significant write-down first.

Selective asset presentation: Corporates only publish pictures of their best assets on the front cover of their annual reports or investor presentations.

Doubtful sector classification: The same asset being classified as industrial with one company, only for it later to be labelled as an office by the new owner, as the price would be higher with the latter classification.

Muddling with accountancy measures: For example, WeWork used a community adjusted EBITDA (standing for earnings before interest, tax, depreciation and amortisation), but also adjusted for all kinds of costs, such as marketing, admin and design.

Inconsistent performance measure calculations: There are ten different ways to calculate a performance measure. We already discussed the different yield calculations, but the same problems arise with other measures such as the cost ratio or vacancy (see next box).

Sensational press headlines: At one point, the media reported that a German residential company expected a negative asset revaluation of 30% over 2022–2024, but upon checking, it was its bear case, not the base case.

A bull market masking the real situation: Sub-optimal companies can perform well versus the sector if their assets are well sought after by the market. However, as Alan Carter says: 'Never confuse their genius with a bull market'. It is, therefore, important to analyse the valuation drivers in detail, compare with sector peers and understand what is happening behind the scenes, because one day fortunes will change. To repeat Warren Buffett's famous quote: 'Only when the tide goes out do you learn who has been swimming naked'.[1]

Ten Different Ways to Calculate a Performance Measure...

When I was part of the European Public Real Estate Association (EPRA) Accountancy Committee, I had the honour of leading the initiatives to set the best practice rules for calculating the EPRA

Net Initial Yield and the EPRA Cost Ratio, among others. It was a real eye-opener: there are so many ways to calculate a performance measure! The differences created by including or excluding an item in the numerator or denominator can have a significant impact. Over the years, I have learned to scrutinise these numbers carefully, as everyone chooses the most favourable way of calculating if they can.

In addition, in Europe, there are so many country and cultural differences that it often took a long time to develop a harmonised measure. This was mainly because CFOs feared being unfairly compared to peers in other countries with different rental markets and tax systems.

Let's have a closer look at two EPRA performance measures: the cost ratio and vacancy. These may seem simple to calculate, but they can be done in very different ways!

EPRA Cost Ratio

The calculation of the cost ratio looks simple in principle, but there are many different interpretations possible. Which costs should go through the profit and loss (P&L) account and which can be capitalised through equity? How can a cost ratio be compared between certain countries? (Answer: with difficulty, as in some countries tenants pay for utilities while in others they do not, and there are differences in taxes as well, none of which indicate the efficiency of the manager.) Should the cost ratio use gross rental income as a denominator or total assets, and what exactly should be included? The debate goes on and on.

In fact, the debate about how to determine the cost ratio completely escalated within the EPRA Accountancy Committee and required intervention from the board. It resulted in the recommendation to publish two cost ratios: one including the cost of vacancy and the other excluding the cost of vacancy. Additionally, the recommendation includes a note that cost ratios of listed companies in different jurisdictions are not always comparable. Furthermore, a

(Continued)

(Continued)

detailed cost table should be provided so analysts and investors can make adjustments if they have a different view.

Simply put, under the EPRA definition, companies should include all administrative and operating expenses in the IFRS statements, including the share of joint ventures minus any service fees. These costs should be expressed as a percentage of the gross rental income (minus ground rents).

EPRA Vacancy

The determination of the vacancy rate is also an interesting one to mention. Is it based on square metres? If the remaining space that is vacant is actually more expensive (i.e. will attract a higher rent than the currently let space), this method of calculating vacancy would underestimate the 'real' vacancy. So, is it better to express vacancy in rent? But what is the rent of vacant space? If one assumes a low rent for the vacant space while using the current contracted rent for the let space, vacancy will be underestimated again.

The recommended way of estimating the EPRA vacancy is by dividing the estimated rental value (ERV) or the expected rent of letting the space today at market rent of the vacant space by the ERV of the whole portfolio. This definition also leaves room for different interpretations, but I agree with EPRA that this is the most optimal one.

Focus on Cash Flow

Property company financial statements are sometimes full of non-cash items. For example, under IFRS, real estate valuations are included in the P&L account, even though they are not realised. Sir Stelios Haji-Ioannou, who is well known for founding the budget airline easyJet and easyHotel, said to me: 'Lots of people focus on unrealised gains and losses. I focus on [cash] dividends and realised gains'. Additionally, the reported rental income is not equal to the real cash collected because incentives, such

Scrutinise Property Investment Vehicles

as a rent-free period, are streamlined over the length of the contract. For instance, if a tenant commits to paying a rent of 100 per year for ten years and receives one-year rent-free, the cash flow for the landlord would be 0 in year one and 100 in the remaining nine years. However, the accounts will show 90 per year (100 minus a 10% discount).

Another issue is that certain items are arbitrary; e.g. maintenance capital expenditure (capex) can be quite easily moved between reporting years or, in some cases, charged straight through equity and not through the P&L. I can mention many other issues, such as capitalised interest, but the point is that the P&L account should be carefully scrutinised. This can be done by making adjustments, but one simple way is to closely examine the cash flow statement as well. In the end, the cash flow is the heart of the business and shows what the dividend payment potential is (or is not). Jaap Tonckens, the former CFO of Unibail-Rodamco-Westfield (URW), told me years ago that many analysts focus too much on the accountancy P&L whilst completely ignoring the cash flow. A missed opportunity.

Scrutinising the IVG Investment Case

One of the high-flyers of European real estate before the Global Financial Crisis (GFC) (and still a bit into it) was the German real estate company IVG Immobilien. Everybody seemed to love the investment case. It was all about 'caverns, caverns and caverns'. A real hype. No other real estate company owned this type of asset, which is used for underground storage of natural gas and crude oil. In 2007, IVG owned 40 of these caverns, with another 90 in its development pipeline. The more caverns they could build, the better. Some analysts even fantasised about the potential of building a cavern below an existing cavern and the upside this would result in. Unfortunately, they could not.

However, both I and my colleague Osmaan Malik, who was the main analyst on the stock, did not understand the hype. In November 2007, we published a deep dive in which Osmaan scrutinised the company in detail: the cavern business looked

(Continued)

(Continued)

exciting indeed, but we believed too much development profit was already accounted for, which we felt was also the case for its commercial property development portfolio. Additionally, we expected its fund management business to slow down. We downgraded the stock to 'Underweight'.

It was a contrarian call at that time. We were summoned to their office to explain our reasoning. While they disagreed with our research, we left even more convinced of our case than we were before. Next, we met a high-flying executive from one of the largest hedge funds at the time. He looked like he had literally just stepped off his yacht. For him, IVG was the hottest real estate company out there, but that view changed after meeting us.

The more we dug through the report, the more red flags we found, such as excessive asset valuations and development profits brought forward years before completion. We continued to downgrade the price target over the next few years and maintained our Underweight rating. From 2012 onwards, Tim Leckie, now the main analyst on the stock, set our price target very close to zero, and we remained sellers. This was not going to end well.

The company began a painful decline, as there was too much 'blue sky' priced in for its business lines, including the caverns. Additionally, it was hit by valuation declines in both the investment and development portfolio, with their major 660-metre-long project, the Squaire next to Frankfurt airport, being a major challenge. This mega office and hotel development suffered from delays and cost overruns (cost of circa €1 billion versus a budget of €660 million), while it was hard to fill the 146,000 square metre property. In the end, tenants such as KPMG and Hilton signed up, but not on the anticipated terms. I estimated that the valuation of the building was circa 30% below cost in the summer of 2013 (if it could be sold at all), when the company was fighting for survival. In August 2013, IVG asked for insolvency protection, and the story ended on 14 August 2014, with its last day of trading on the 13th.

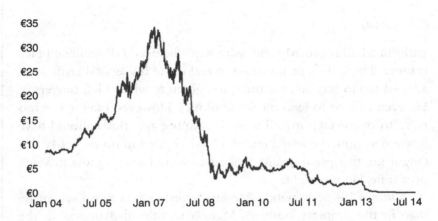

Figure 13.1 IVG Immobilien AG – share price
Source: Adapted from FactSet.

Mosaic Theory

I am a big believer in the Mosaic theory: gathering lots of information (puzzle pieces) from different sources, e.g. financial statistics, company data, management, results conference calls (particularly the Q&A part), property agents, site visits, competing companies, shareholders, analysts, etc., to come to an investment recommendation (solve the puzzle). Of course, this should not include the use of insider information.

In particular, I recommend having contacts with the older gurus who have seen it all. As Rutger van der Lubbe, Head of Global Real Estate Investment Strategy at APG Asset Management, told me: 'Wisdom comes with the years'. That truly enriches you, helps you grasp situations, and gives you the guts to take an (opposite) market view or position.

Note that the analysis of a company, fund or portfolio is never really finished. One must remain critical and continuously ask: 'Why?' It is an infinite question that arises after every researched answer.

My First Gurus

I finished my degree in 1998 and had my mind set on Amsterdam. The housing market was so hot that I had to settle for a room

(Continued)

(Continued)

without a bathroom. My dad, who was a beloved GP (general practitioner) but had made investing in real estate his second profession, advised me to buy an apartment straightaway when I left university. He even offered to lend me some money. However, I felt it was too risky to overstretch myself at such a young age. But I should have listened to him: the apartment doubled in price in no time. My dad taught me that good quality real estate would always grow in value over time. He was right.

One of his best friends, Menno Smitsloo, was a real self-made man in the property business. Menno was the first person in the Netherlands to start a real estate brokerage purely for commercial property, became very successful, sold it and now runs a successful family business (with a royal label) focused on investing in and managing real estate. In a newspaper, he was once quoted saying: 'In anticipation of better times, many entrepreneurs have put their policies on the back burner. But better times don't come by themselves; you must make them. And of course, that won't work if everyone throws in the towel. Should a good plan be put on hold because a few faint-hearted people are talking each other into a crisis? No way!'[2] I like his way of thinking.

His advice as a seasoned property investor is second to none. For example, when borrowing costs were still low at the beginning of 2022 and financial markets started to wonder how high they could rise, he was very clear when I spoke with him: 'They are way too low, they should be more like 5%'. For him, it was so obvious. He even mentioned it in a sub-sentence of something else we were talking about, as if it were a given. He would be proven right months later. It is so valuable for investors to have access to successful property veterans. You never stop learning from them.

Notes

1. Warren Buffet (1993) 'Berkshire Hathaway 1992 Shareholder Letter,' 1 March.
2. *Leidsch Dagblad*, 25 July 1991, p. 13.

Chapter 14

Significant Upside Based on Multicriteria Valuations

The goal is to find those stocks that have significant upside based on multiple valuation metrics under various scenarios (bear/base/bull case). This is not a book on valuation specifically, but it provides a basic overview of my preferred approach.

Historical Performance Analysis

The initial step involves analysing the historical performance of the shares in comparison to their peers, i.e. similar businesses. This entails examining how the shares behaved over various periods, both in absolute terms and relative to others. What factors contributed to the shares' returns being better or worse? Were there specific events that influenced their performance? How did the stock fare in particular situations? What was the sensitivity of the share price? This straightforward analysis can already offer valuable insights into the company. For instance, the shares might

128 REAL ESTATE RULES

have exhibited exceptional volatility during turbulent times compared to similar businesses, possibly due to higher financial leverage or weaker portfolio positioning.

Six Basic Valuation Metrics

There are several straightforward metrics that can provide a first impression of a stock's valuation. The ultimate goal is to identify a stock that scores well across all measures, is cheaper than its peers, and trades at more favourable levels than its historical averages.

Here, we discuss six valuation metrics: discount to net asset value (NAV), dividend yield, earnings yield, implied EBITDA yield, discount to gross asset value (GAV), and implied price per square metre. Appendix II includes a table that outlines the definition and calculation method for each metric. It is important to note that the first three metrics consider leverage, while the last three are ungeared. Furthermore, I provide only the simplified calculation. Adjustments can often be made to refine the measure; e.g. one could adjust for deferred taxes, derivatives and goodwill in the NAV calculation, or exclude non-cash items from earnings per share (EPS).

It is essential to recognise that each metric only captures one aspect of the business. For instance, the discount to NAV reflects the discount to book equity based on the most recent appraisal. However, this metric does not provide insight into the cost structure, financing mix, tax regime, quality of management, corporate governance, or the outlook for the assets. Moreover, the appraisal valuation might be outdated. NAV is probably the most widely used, lagging/smoothed/biased and (therefore) criticised measure. It is true that certain market participants, especially companies, are too fixated on it, which can hamper growth aspirations as they do not want to raise equity at a discount to NAV, which itself is out of date. As Jaap Tonckens says: 'The narrow focus on NAV for valuing companies is valuation by the lazy for the lazy'. However, it still has some value if one understands the context and makes adjustments.

Therefore, for the best results, these metrics should be considered collectively. Even then, it is important to exercise caution, as a high score across all metrics might still indicate a company of poor quality, necessitating further adjustments.

Significant Upside Based on Multicriteria Valuations 129

Despite this, one can draw interesting preliminary conclusions. For example:

- A stock trading at a low earnings yield but a wide discount to NAV might suggest that the NAV is overstated or that the company is poorly managed, indicated by a high cost ratio.
- If the dividend yield exceeds the earnings yield, it implies the company is paying out more than it earns, which is usually unsustainable in the long term, especially if leverage is high.
- A high discount to NAV, but not to GAV, indicates significant leverage within the company.
- A high earnings yield coupled with a low EBITDA yield could point to high leverage and a low cost of debt.

Example

Many investors assess real estate stocks using only a limited number of valuation metrics, such as discount to NAV and dividend yield. This narrow approach often results in poor investments and can be a recipe for disaster. Let's look at an example (Table 14.1).

Table 14.1 Selecting an investment based on six valuation metrics – example

	Investment 1	Investment 2	Investment 3
Discount to NAV	50%	40%	30%
Dividend yield	1.5%	5.5%	5.1%
Earnings yield	1.7%	5.0%	6.8%
Implied EBITDA yield	5.1%	5.6%	6.2%
Discount to GAV	18%	20%	23%
Implied price per sq. m (€)	2,475	2,400	2,325

Source: Author.

Assume an investor is contemplating investing in one of three companies with similar portfolios. This is what typically happens. Based only on the discount to NAV (first row), Investment 1 would be chosen. However, if the dividend yield (second row) is included, the preference would switch to Investment 2, as the discount is still high but it offers a much higher dividend yield compared to Investment 1. Nevertheless, the

130   REAL ESTATE RULES

cheapest and least risky stock is Investment 3. By including the EPS yield in the analysis (third row), we see that not only does Investment 2 have a lower earnings yield than Investment 3, but also that its dividend yield is higher than its earnings yield, which means it is paying out more than it earns. Additionally, the last three metrics show that Investment 3 performs better once corrected for leverage: it has a higher EBITDA yield (implied portfolio yield after overhead costs), a higher discount to the portfolio value and the lowest implied price per square metre. A review of the company accounts would reveal that Investment 3 has lower financial leverage, a better cost ratio, a lower cost of debt and the most sensible dividend payout ratio (Table 14.2).

Table 14.2   Company positioning – input example

	Investment 1	Investment 2	Investment 3
Yield on portfolio*	6%	6%	6%
Loan-to-value	65%	50%	25%
Cost ratio	30%	25%	20%
Cost of debt	6%	6%	5%
Dividend payout	90%	110%	75%

*Defined as gross rent divided by portfolio value.

Source: Author.

A couple of rules of thumb:

- Well-managed companies active in booming markets tend to trade at a premium to NAV (share price is above NAV, as the equity market expects future values to rise and management to add value), whilst poorly managed companies in declining markets tend to trade at wide discounts to NAV.
- A discount to NAV of 40% or more is typically a strong buying opportunity if the NAV is not forecast to fall significantly and debt covenants are not in danger. In other cases, it is most likely a sign that the company is not optimally positioned or that something is seriously wrong.
- Quality companies trading at a discount to GAV of more than 15% could be interesting to consider (if everything else is in check).
- If the dividend payout (dividend divided by recurring earnings) is higher than 85%, the company typically pays out too much in cash, as

Significant Upside Based on Multicriteria Valuations   131

it is not provisioning for capital expenditure (capex). Ideally, this ratio should be closer to 75%, but it also depends on the type of assets, balance sheet and capital commitments.

Modelling

The valuation metrics not only have their specific shortcomings, but they also ignore asset quality, rent and earnings growth outlook, capital expenditure, potential management improvements and any value add. These measures can be combined with risk or growth outlook, e.g. by calculating an adjusted ratio such as the price earnings-to-growth (PEG) ratio, where the earnings are divided by the growth rate. Alternatively, one can construct a more comprehensive valuation model, such as a Dividend Discount Model (DDM) or a Discounted Cash Flow Model (DCFM). However, the accuracy of these models relies on assumptions and forecasts, which might be incorrect. Additionally, certain models might not be suitable for certain stocks; e.g. a DDM works well for steady dividend-paying stocks but is tricky to apply to high-growth stocks and developers.

My preferred approach:

i. Valuation of portfolio (and resulting NAV) by myself

Given the shortcomings of the published company NAV, such as its lagging nature and potential bias, I estimate the portfolio value myself using a five-year DCFM. The model input is based on:

- Company data available, such as rental income, lease expiration schedule, any contractual rental uplifts, under/over-renting of the assets and (expected) capital expenditure.
- My market rental growth outlook, based on my direct market models, such as the previously discussed office model.
- My forecast discount rate, based on real-time market data such as long-term government and corporate bond yields, swap rates, prevailing credit spreads and risk premiums.

An adjustment is included if variables are significantly more favourable than long-term averages. For example, one cannot rely on ultra-loose monetary policy indefinitely, as seen after the Global Financial Crisis (GFC), and, hence, should use a higher discount rate than indicated by the current market. Similarly, an exit rate significantly different from its long-term average can only be used if justified by an improved long-term rental growth outlook.

Based on the forecast portfolio value, I calculate my own NAV by deducting the company's net debt from the value and making any other adjustments if I disagree with the company's computation. However, a stock might still trade at a premium or discount to this estimate because the NAV does not take into account whether management is creating value. I address this in the next step.

ii. EVA model for estimating discount or premium to NAV

The EVA model can explain which parts of the business are underperforming (resulting in a discount) or performing well (premium). Essentially, if a company has a low ROIC due to a relatively high cost structure and high cost of capital, its EVA spread (ROIC − WACC) is negative, indicating it is destroying capital. I prefer to forecast five years of EVA, multiply each year's spread by the capital employed (net debt plus estimated book equity), discount the value-add back to today and then add or subtract from the NAV calculated in the first step. Figure 14.1 shows that I start with the reported NAV per share, which I then estimate myself and subsequently adjust with EVA for any value creation or destruction.

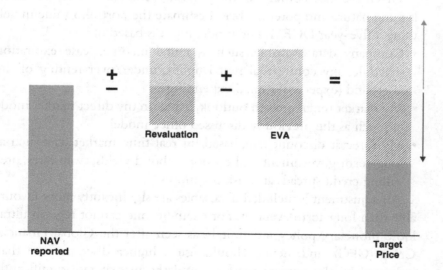

Figure 14.1 Author preferred company valuation: adjust NAV and add EVA
Source: Author.

Unconventional Reasons Why Listed Real Estate Companies Can Trade at a Discount to the Appraisal NAV

Clearly, property companies can trade at a discount to NAV if they are not optimally positioned, e.g. due to a high-cost structure, poor management or a weak balance sheet. However, there can also be unconventional reasons:

- Valuations of listed companies are real-time and, therefore, exhibit a change in trend much earlier. Based on my experience, the underlying property market lags the listed markets by around six to eight months and even longer during a downturn. Valuers typically wait to adjust property values until there is ample evidence (concept of willing buyer and willing seller), but this process takes time during times of trouble. Additionally, real estate portfolios are usually externally valued only once or twice a year, and some appraisers have a tendency to 'smooth' valuations over time, particularly in certain jurisdictions when property values are falling.
- Listed company pricing can be impacted in the short term by media, analyst reports, a single macro data point or simply the mood of the day. For example, in 2022, the financial community anticipated a severe recession, which never materialised. This affected sentiment and depressed share prices (further).
- Share prices can be influenced by technicalities, including stocks being included or excluded from benchmarks, derivatives hedging/expirations and the rebalancing of investment strategies. For example, some funds follow a strict 60% equities and 40% bonds policy, resulting in frequent portfolio rebalancing.
- If real estate is not in vogue, a limited number of investors care. Different groups of investors are active in the listed market, with varying risk/return requirements. Private investors, institutions (e.g. pension funds and insurance companies) and dedicated real estate investors typically have lower return expectations, while general equity investors and hedge funds seek higher returns.

(Continued)

134   REAL ESTATE RULES

(Continued)

The latter two groups look at the entire market universe, selecting the best opportunities. If tech is hot, they invest in tech; if pharmacy, they invest in pharmacy; if real estate, they invest in real estate. If not real estate, they hold underweight or no positions, or even short the sector, betting on falling share prices. This results in share price fluctuations (volatility) and periods where the sector can either be in favour with everybody or completely out of favour, perhaps due to a downturn or the emergence of another 'hot' sector like dot-com companies at the end of the 1990s. It could also be because the outlook for real estate is unexciting, e.g. real estate prices are expected to remain stable, which deters investors: 'I'll see you again when there is action!'

- Listed real estate is the 'piggy bank' of the sector. Because listed real estate is liquid, investors can quickly gain exposure to a new trend in the property market or sell their holdings to free up cash. When a downturn hits, it is difficult, if not impossible, to sell properties in the underlying market. Frequently, there are simply no buyers during these dark moments, or they only buy at ridiculously low prices. As a result, listed real estate runs a higher risk of being sold, as it offers cash instantaneously, but this can also lead to share prices falling more than they should, based on fundamentals: they overshoot to the downside. This is not ideal, but at least listed real estate offers liquidity.

Invest with Margin for Error

Valuation models are useful to have, but their outcomes depend on the input. Garbage in, garbage out! Nobody has a crystal ball into the future, so we should always realise that the model's output is based on assumptions. I tend to rely on my model outputs, but I continuously fine-tune the inputs based on our research and market feedback and include a 'margin for error' in the models, similar to direct property valuations. For example, I would reduce rental growth expectations or increase the discount rate to a level I am certain is very conservative. If the valuation upside is still significant and the company does not have any problems

Significant Upside Based on Multicriteria Valuations

with its debt covenants or financing in general, the stock is likely to be a comfortable Buy. Similarly, I like to see how the valuation upside changes under different input scenarios (from very bearish to very bullish) to assess the risk/return profile of a stock. Are expected returns more weighted to the upside or downside?

Clearly, the bigger the margin for error in the model, the better. Ideally, one invests when all variables are favourable: high yield, low rental levels (high expected growth), high risk premium, high interest rates, etc.

Chapter 15

Focus on (Upcoming) Value Creators, Be Careful with Destroyers

Valuation is one thing, but company positioning (or momentum) is another. There can be two stocks with similar upside, but one might be active in a terrible market with poor management, while the other is in a flourishing market with great prospects and top-notch management. Most likely, estimates for the former would have to be downgraded in the future, whereas those for the latter would be upgraded, e.g. due to better-than-expected rental growth and higher-than-expected profitability from acquisitions and developments (and vice versa for the former). Companies with positive momentum are on an upward spiral of success, while those with negative momentum are on a downward spiral of doom.

To achieve optimal results, investors should aim to find those stocks that have good valuation upside and have the potential to fire on as many cylinders as possible. These are strong value creators, well-positioned for current investment themes,[1] and have a good number of upcoming share price catalysts. Stocks that are 'stuck' or 'fighting for survival' should be ignored unless they are extremely cheap on multiple metrics, have good quality assets, a bulletproof balance sheet and are expected to see improved momentum or a turnaround at some stage.

Introducing a Framework: Get on the Right Highway!

It is crucial that the company is on the right path: the upward spiral of success (the right half of Figure 15.1), and not on the vicious downward spiral of doom (the left half of Figure 15.1). Companies on the upward highway of success have their house in order and strive to optimise the business at all times with a goal of 'firing on all cylinders'. The more levers a company can pull, the more value creation and the higher the share price. High-quality companies are moving along this route of success. This is the main hunting ground for investors, ideally at the end of the potential phase or the beginning of the 'firing on all cylinders' phase.

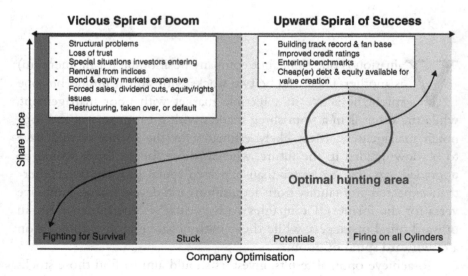

Figure 15.1 Goal to fire on all cylinders
Source: Author.

Focus on (Upcoming) Value Creators, Be Careful with Destroyers 139

Things start to become problematic if companies are (or end up) on the vicious downward spiral. These businesses have structural issues; e.g. the assets are not future proof, the balance sheet is not secure, management is out of touch, transparency is poor and/or alignment between shareholders and executives is sub-optimal or non-existent. Drastic action is needed to change course and return to the road of success. The longer the structural issues persist, the bigger the problem becomes. The market (and the company's other stakeholders) will lose trust every day, which will be increasingly hard to repair. The worse the situation, the higher the cost of repair. Investors who pick stocks on the downward spiral should be convinced that the situation will be turned around and that the valuation more than compensates for the risk taken. This is often not the case: other unforeseen negative events occur, time eats into returns, and a stock re-rating, if it happens at all, only occurs after the shares have been completely beaten down.

Within the upward spiral of success are two phases: (a) firing on all cylinders and (b) potentials; and within the vicious spiral of doom: (c) stuck and (d) fighting for survival.

(a) Firing on All Cylinders

At the top of the spiral, in the firing on all cylinders phase, companies are fully optimised and underlying markets are booming, resulting in superior rental and capital growth, efficiencies and value creation. The shares trade at a premium valuation and generally attract wide(r) investor interest, including hedge funds and general equity investors. Nicholas Vetch, Executive Chairman of self-storage company Big Yellow, aptly put it during an analyst meeting in 2011: 'I will bet a lunch in a good restaurant that the stock market will value this business higher than the real estate market will do (somewhere) in the next years', as he foresaw that his business would be 'firing on all cylinders'. Corporates in this category are building a track record and a fan base, improving their credit ratings, entering equity benchmarks and having cheaper debt and equity available for value creation activities, such as acquisitions, mergers and acquisitions (M&A) and development. This is where companies should aim to be. In the firing on all cylinders phase, companies create superior shareholder value, and investors should aim to invest in this category ideally at the start of this phase.

140 REAL ESTATE RULES

Stocks in the firing on all cylinders phase are strong value creators, have the right investment theme and numerous share price catalysts:

i. Strong value creation

These companies have an attractive investment story and are not just 'sitting on the assets'. Think about generating superior rental growth, establishing a leading platform, acquiring assets or companies with a low cost of capital, rolling out a development pipeline in an undersupplied market, optimising costs, obtaining investment-grade status, strategic repositioning in a different real estate segment, or even a turnaround, creating a cluster of assets, etc. Stocks in the firing on all cylinders phase have a high positive EVA spread.

Real Estate	Balance Sheet	Management & Governance
• Demand/supply fundamentals • Long-term trends (e.g. ESG) • Sector/country/micro • Capex • Value-add initiatives	• Bullet-proof • Sources of financing • Maturity profile • Dividend policy	• Strategy • Transparency • Alignment • Accountability • Cost ratios • Tax

Examples of levers for value creation
Source: Author.

ii. Right theme

These stocks are well positioned in terms of investment themes/trends for a sustained period, e.g. if the theme is artificial intelligence (AI) (then data centres), e-commerce (logistics), real estate downturn (low leverage, long debt maturity, secure income, limited development), low emissions (low carbon portfolio), etc.

iii. Catalysts

The shares have numerous share price triggers, i.e. positive news flow that can boost the share price: better-than-expected results, announcement of a new strategy, new top management, obtaining an improved credit rating, increased dividends, special dividends, profitable acquisitions, successful portfolio sales, signing new tenants, opening new developments, development lettings, stock entering a benchmark, etc. Stocks on the other side of the spectrum, i.e. in the fighting for survival phase, face negative catalysts, e.g. worse-than-expected results, dividend cuts, highly discounted equity raises, upcoming debt expirations in a difficult market, and so on.

Big Yellow: Continuously Optimising the Business

Big Yellow is a UK storage company I have always admired, because its managers, Nicholas Vetch, Executive Chairman, and Jim Gibson, CEO, are always thoughtful about their business and are continuously working to optimise it further. They built up the business from scratch starting in 1998 (together with Philip Burks) and brought it to the stock exchange in 2000. The chairman at that time said: 'You will work hard, you will earn your luck'. That is what they did and that is what happened. Like most successful businesses, they found an underdeveloped niche with strong demand/supply dynamics. However, the consumer-facing business was loss-making until 2003 (profitable in 2004).

Of course, not everything went according to plan. Big Yellow was first called Storage Stuff, but having realised that many people associated 'Stuff' with 'Drugs', they eventually changed the name to Big Yellow. The venture was successful from the beginning, but during the Great Financial Crisis (GFC), they learned that finance is not always available, even for them. But Big Yellow secured new capital when Lehman fell over and had to suspend its dividend for 18 months. That was a lesson for the successful start-up. 'You don't want analysts writing about you that you could go bust because you cannot refinance!'

I always enjoy Nicholas's commentary during analyst meetings. One quote I noted down in 2012 (the recovery years after GFC): 'We are currently between paranoia and acceleration [for the Big Yellow business]'. He was right; everybody was gloomy and paranoid, but the storage business would (continue to) flourish in the years to come.

In Nicholas and Jim's philosophy, a real estate investment trust (REIT) should focus on growing income, high dividend distribution and low financial gearing – in their case, an loan-to-value (LTV) of 10–15% and net debt to EBITDA of up to 3.5 times (with therefore low share price volatility). It is about compounding returns and consistency. It is not about financial engineering and endless discussions with valuers about the value of assets in the books (and its resultant NAV).

But Be Careful When Expectations Become Unrealistic

Whilst the firing on all cylinders phase is the holy grail for companies and investors alike, one should realise that at some point the party will end. When it does, it is crucial that the company does not slip back into the danger zone on the vicious downward spiral with disastrous performance consequences. Unfortunately, many companies in this phase are not well prepared for setbacks or become overconfident, e.g. by taking on too much debt, assuming financing will always be available or engaging in speculative development. Remember: real estate is cyclical, and valuations can become unrealistically high. The stock market can get so excited that the share price rockets to a level where profit expectations become unsustainable for the long term, or the margin for error becomes too low. This is an accident waiting to happen.

The Reload Factor

Russian development companies were 'hot' in the period before the GFC. Investors fell in love with these companies so much that the prices of some of these developers could only be justified if one included a so-called reload factor in the valuation model. This meant that investors were prepared to pay not only for ongoing development projects but also for future projects that did not yet exist. Investors who went on property trips to Russia were shown pieces of land with apparently great prospects, but it required a lot of imagination. Dirk Philippa recalls: 'In 2005, I attended a property tour in Moscow. It was one of the most bizarre tours I have been on. We skipped the lines at the airport by using the diplomatic line and had a police escort to the city centre. You realise this is an insiders' market, so not for us! It was one of the least transparent property markets, but the key issue was that the rule of law could be stretched, which makes enforcing a rental contract difficult or the [development] process unpredictable'. Indeed, it would end badly, with share prices going down to almost zero or zero.

VGP: Don't Assume Financing Will Always Be There

VGP NV, a successful pan-European owner, manager and developer of logistics and semi-industrial real estate, was firing on all cylinders until it wasn't. It just managed to avoid disaster, but at a significant cost. Its shares generated a whopping shareholder return of 2,139% (25% annualised) from the end of 2007 to its peak in 2021. Everything went well. Logistics was in vogue, with demand for VGP's product running red hot. Financing was widely available. In April 2021, VGP successfully issued its first public green bond for €600 million with an eight-year maturity, paying a coupon of only 1.50%. In November 2021, it raised €300 million in fresh equity at €240 per share, close to its all-time high share price. So far, so good.

It had done a great job but made one expensive mistake: it assumed financing would always be available. It was – until it wasn't. It had counted on its joint venture partner Allianz and the financial markets. However, when sentiment drastically turned in 2022, as interest rates started to rise and investment appetite for real estate dropped, it was in trouble. It could no longer find cheap capital for funding its (ongoing) development projects. VGP got hit. As a result, its green bonds were trading at much higher yields, reaching just above 10% on 28 October 2022, which meant that a bond was valued at approximately 60 versus its face value of 100, i.e. 40% lower. Its share price suddenly went into a tailspin, plummeting more than 70% from its November high (see Figure 15.2). Much of the historically hard-earned returns were destroyed in no time (although its annualised total shareholder return is still a respectable c. 14% since 2007 until September 2024). In November 2022, it announced a highly dilutive rights issue for approximately €300 million at a price per share of €55.50, roughly a 35% discount to the previous closing price and 77% discount to the equity raise a year earlier. The theoretical ex-rights price (TERP) was approximately €79 (measured by adding the market value of the shares before the rights issue announcement plus the rights issue amount, divided by the new total number of shares after the rights issue). Although at a high cost, VGP had brought the downward spiral to a standstill and moved out of the value destruction zone.

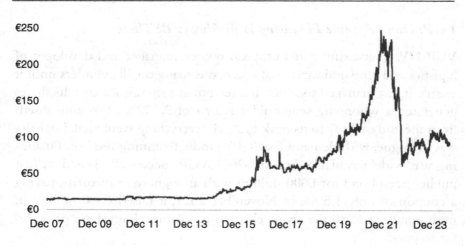

Figure 15.2 VGP NV – share price
Source: FactSet.

(b) Potentials

At the start of the upward spiral are companies whose business models are intact but not yet optimised. For example, the asset class might be temporarily out of favour, management may not have fully optimised the business yet or it still needs to prove itself. However, their situation is expected to improve in the near future. These companies typically start to re-rate once their sector focus comes into vogue and/or the company begins to bear fruit from an ambitious business plan. Companies in the potentials phase are trading 'okayish' but mainly attract interest from dedicated real estate and local investors. However, stocks in this category are attractive M&A targets because of their return potential once they enter the firing on all cylinders phase. Private equity firms like Blackstone, Brookfield and TPG have been active acquirers of listed companies over the years. The potentials category is, therefore, an attractive hunting ground to uncover tomorrow's rising stars.

(c) Stuck

If the company is not optimally positioned, e.g. due to governance issues, management shortcomings or business optimisation failures, and this situation persists for some time, the shares are priced at a significant discount. As a result, public debt and equity markets are often more expensive or may even be closed, hampering growth and future value creation. Initially, there are a few hopeful shareholders, such as smaller local general equity investors, dedicated property investors or private investors, who believe that things will improve. However, after limited improvements or outright disappointments, frustration sets in. Discontent grows among shareholders, management, the board and employees.

Drastic change is needed to get onto the upward spiral of success. This may include deleveraging (e.g. selling assets), asset rotation, a new (sustainable) dividend policy, new management (and board) and better alignment with shareholder interests. These companies and their investors are 'stuck' until a significant shift happens. The shares trade at a discount indefinitely, go nowhere, and most of these companies eventually launch a (forced) strategic review and/or are taken over after a painful period when nobody was genuinely happy with each other. The potential takeover does not only happen after a long time, but the take-out price is also often lower than anticipated.

Investing in this category is only worthwhile if (a) change is really happening and has a high chance of being successful or (b) there is a significant percentage of shareholders pushing for change (around 25%) and the board is likely to listen and act. Otherwise, be careful not to get stuck in an investment with disappointing returns.

Speed Up or Find a Bride

In 2001, I published my first research note on high street shop specialist Vastned Retail, titled 'Speed up or find a bride'. We initiated with a Reduce rating, advising investors to sell the shares, as we doubted the performance of the German portfolio and urged management to take action. The company made gradual changes, but I could have written a similar note with the same title in 2023, as it would take until 2024 to see drastic changes.

Figure 15.3 Vastned Retail – share price
Source: Factset.

(d) Fighting for Survival

Unfortunately, not many companies move from the 'stuck' category up to the spiral of success, as management teams and boards are often ignorant, passive or even reluctant to make changes. This reluctance might stem from managers earning good money or having a 'blind spot' about a potential downside scenario. Worse still, companies in the 'stuck' phase run a high risk of escalating into the fighting-for-survival phase. This can happen due to a significant (unexpected) change in trend, a (macro) shock to the system or a critical analyst/short seller report. In this phase, things go from bad to worse. One should expect the unexpected: analyst downgrades (or even suspended ratings), margin calls for leveraged stock investors, credit rating downgrades, bond and equity markets closing (or worse: banks/bond markets forcing a deeply discounted equity issue or restructuring), dropping out of equity indices, negative press reports, disappointing company results, potential lawsuits, special situation investors (including short sellers and hedge funds) entering the scene, regulatory investigations, etc.

The business model is often broken beyond repair. The company is fighting for survival, which frequently ends in a painful and costly restructuring (cost-cutting, minimising capital expenditure, forced sales, dividend cuts and equity/rights issues), takeover or default. Trust is destroyed among all the stakeholders. The 'fan' base, if it ever existed, has mostly left, but some remain, seeing the stock as having 'optional' value now. They believe

Focus on (Upcoming) Value Creators, Be Careful with Destroyers 147

that the share price is so low that it hardly matters if it goes to zero: perhaps someone will come along and bid a premium, or a miracle will happen that makes the stock rebound. But that is often wishful thinking. Companies ending up in the 'fighting for survival' phase need to take drastic action as soon as possible before things escalate out of control. Many companies act too late and ultimately fail.

Investing in these companies is not for the faint-hearted, as a significant number of companies do not survive, and if they do, it will be at a high cost. Examples of companies in this category over the period 2021–2024 include Adler Group, SBB and Branicks Group (formerly DIC Asset). Investors in this bracket need to have patience, a deep understanding of the situation and the ability to endure high volatility, as typically more negative surprises materialise than expected and the equity market does not give the benefit of the doubt. Investors can potentially find excessive returns, but the stock would need to be extremely cheap on multiple metrics, have good quality assets, stay out of the hands of debt providers and show improved momentum or a turnaround at some stage.

The Accelerator Effect

Frequently, companies in the 'fighting for survival' phase find it impossible to turn the situation around (and even for those in the 'stuck' phase it is a daunting task), especially when underlying real estate markets hit rougher weather. Most of these businesses also tend to suffer from excessive financial leverage. These two elements are a toxic combination, resulting in an accelerator effect on the already troubling situation. Management has no control over the outcome anymore, and its fate is in the hands of financial markets.

The accelerator effect works as follows. Property prices fall. Banks limit lending while becoming stricter with their current lending book. Numerous other real estate investors are also in trouble and need to sell assets, putting further pressure on property prices, making banks even more cautious and pushing real estate values further down. This can result in an intensifying downward spiral, which is hard to stop and typically overshoots, leaving many casualties and taking significant time to clear. This is what happened during the GFC, until the central banks stepped in to turn the tide by providing ample liquidity to the system.

It is a challenging task to restructure a company with structural issues, let alone a broken business model, in this environment. Many market participants have their own issues, and there are only a limited number of buyers who will exploit their negotiating position to the maximum. Any turnaround will come at a high price or not happen at all, resulting in default. Very few manage to come through this phase unscathed before the real estate market rebounds, but it is possible, albeit more an exception to the rule.

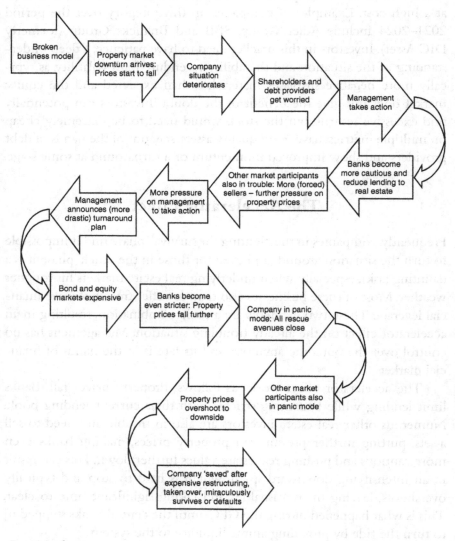

Source: Author.

The situation can accelerate not only to the downside but also to the upside. Companies in the 'firing on all cylinders' phase can almost literally fly to the moon due to (sharply) rising property prices and financial leverage, resulting in a great party. However, regardless of the direction of acceleration, both investors and management teams should be on their toes.

Case Study: Stock Selection

Consider four different stocks (see Table 15.1). Based on valuation upside, one might select stock number 4, but in fact, it is a significant value destroyer. It does not align with the right theme, e.g. high leverage versus low leverage, and has negative upcoming share price catalysts, e.g. forced asset sales or an equity rights issue, low-quality assets and a weak balance sheet. Additionally, there is no sign of a turnaround. This stock is in the fighting-for-survival mode. It should not be selected, as its upside compared to the others is not significant enough, and the risk of failure is too high. The model likely underestimates the risk. One should only buy this stock if the assets are good and it is clear it will survive.

Stock number 3 has good upside, good quality assets and an 'okay' balance sheet, but it is in the stuck phase. It looks like dead money for a long time with no change in sight. Stock number 1 is a very solid investment: a good return and strong momentum on its side. It is in the firing-on-all-cylinders phase and is likely to surprise to the upside in the short term. However, its balance sheet is not optimal and could become an issue if the bull market suddenly stops. Stock number 2 looks the best, as it is well positioned and is likely to move from the potentials phase to firing on all cylinders soon: its value creation, theme and catalysts are expected to improve.

Table 15.1 Stock selection – an example

	Upside	Value Creation	Theme	Catalysts	Asset quality	Balance Sheet	Likelihood of change
Stock 1	25%	★★★	★★★	★★★	★★★	★	Yes; for the worse
Stock 2	45%	★	★	★★	★★★	★★★	Yes; for the better
Stock 3	50%	-★★	★		★★★	★★	No
Stock 4	55%	-★★★	-★★★	-★★★	★	★	No

Source: Author.

Note

1. The investment theme is related to market trends. For example, if interest rates are rising, investors should prefer stocks with higher property yields and low leverage. Conversely, if there is a high risk of a recession, investors should favour stocks with guaranteed long-term income, such as long-term leases to the government, rather than short-term leases to economically sensitive sectors.

Chapter 16

Look for Maximum Pessimism and Maximum Optimism

In terms of market timing, my best investment decisions have been when things were looking too good (for a long time), not to participate, or so negative that it was the right time to buy, knowing that the cycle would eventually turn again (as discussed in Chapter 4) or that sentiment had overshot. This is a common phenomenon in financial markets: they tend to move to extremes, e.g. recession is inevitable (it did not happen), inflation will be out of control for a long time (it lasted only a year), interest rates will go down significantly (they decreased very slowly), etc. It is important to always be on the lookout for the moment of maximum optimism (is everybody super bullish? Who is the marginal buyer?) or maximum pessimism ('we are all going to die'). I am always puzzled why numerous institutions only follow others or invest when

151

times are good, while in a downturn, when share prices are 50% lower and quality stocks can be picked up cheaply, only a limited number of parties are interested.

A Round of Applause

At the end of 2006, when I was at JP Morgan, real estate was hot. Everybody was talking about capital flows, capital flows, capital flows! Real estate prices and stocks could only go one way: up! While we had warned about overheating in real estate and had downgraded the sector months before, we still tried to time the share prices. In a note titled 'Dancing with Wolves', we upgraded our price targets by 19% because of these capital flows. The dealing room loved it. After our presentation on the dealing floor, a round of applause followed. By the end of 2006, many share prices had already come close to their new price targets. It worked! But not for long. Soon the GFC would start. We should have stuck to our fundamental view and not tried to time the share price, which is frankly an impossible thing to do, and it made clients puzzled about our real message.

In 2009, the situation was completely reversed. At the end of February, I upgraded Hammerson to Overweight. The company offered an attractive sustainable dividend yield, and its balance sheet was bulletproof after its recent rights issue. However, nobody cared. I went around the dealing room promoting my investment idea. No interest. Some politely listened, but everyone was downbeat. What a difference from November 2006, when everyone was cheering, but the market would collapse soon thereafter! It turned out we were in fact close to the lows of this downturn, which would be on 9 March 2009. Hammerson's share price would stage an impressive rally: it would roughly double in the next six months.

I was deeply frustrated at that time, as everyone was so negative. In one of our morning notes, I wrote the following:

> We are not quite sure the market realises that we seem to have gone from 'leaving no margin for error in valuations' at the beginning of 2007 to 'we cannot have enough margin for error' right now. In 2006,

one just lowered the yield on a portfolio to 4% and said it was a 'buy'. Nowadays, it seems the assumptions for a sound investment case are that yields should be at least 8%, there should be no danger of breaching covenants (with a wide safety margin on top), there should be no refinancing due within three years, an equity raising and dividend cut are factored in, vacancy will rise by 5%, 10% of tenants will go into default, debt premiums are at an all-time high, and market rents will plummet by at least another 30%. And when there is still share price upside after this exercise, the reasoning is that we must be missing something! This may all be true, but it gives a feeling of unmitigated gloom. Just as in 2007 when there was no margin for error and nobody could see the needle that would burst the bubble (but it came!), this could happen now, but the other way around.

Chapter 17

Ensure Management, the Board and Other Shareholders Are Aligned with Investment Objectives

If the management, board and other shareholders do not share the same vision for the company's future as you do, there is a risk of being stuck with an underperforming share. Changing these incentives, removing them or working with opposing investors can be extremely challenging. Therefore, conducting a proper assessment of the situation before investing is crucial.

Management and Board Alignment

A careful analysis is needed, in particular of the following.

Skin in the Game

Numerous successful corporations have management teams with a significant shareholding in the company. They have invested their own money in the business. From my experience, it is generally a positive sign if the top management has a really sizeable position (both relative and absolute) in the company, especially if they are also the founders. The bigger, the better. Of course, there are always exceptions, e.g. when a CEO holds such a high stake but acts purely in their own interest and not in the interest of all shareholders. However, if I create a simple random index of real estate companies where top management has a significant sizeable stake in the company and compare it to the European Public Real Estate Association (EPRA) Europe benchmark index, the outperformance is enormous: 633% versus 73% for the EPRA benchmark since 2008 until end of September 2024, or an annualised 12.6% versus 3.3% (Figure 17.1). While this is by no means an academic analysis and one can debate the index constituents, the performance aligns with my intuitive expectations.

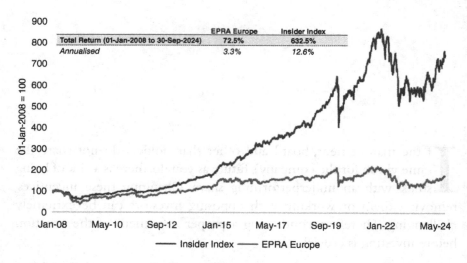

Figure 17.1 European insider-owned REITs vs. EPRA Europe – total return
Source: FactSet; Insider Index is comprised of Altarea, Big Yellow, Lok'nStore, CTP, Industrials REIT, Aroundtown, Frey, VGP, WDP, Montea, and Xior.

Ensure Alignment with Objectives

Incentives in Compensation Packages

As we observed in Chapter 12, incentives can sometimes encourage sub-optimal behaviour or even lead to detrimental outcomes. It is crucial to evaluate whether the performance measures align with shareholder interests, have appropriately challenging targets and cannot be gamed.

Externally or Internally Managed

Externally managed companies are overseen by a third party that receives a fee for its services. Most companies, however, are internally managed, meaning the management team is part of the company, which I prefer. Unfortunately, I have seen many externally managed business models underperform or fail. Only a few have been success stories.

Externally managed companies typically enter the equity market when the market is generally favourable or when they offer something specific that is not widely available, such as a niche property sector or a relatively high dividend yield. The problem is that the alignment between external managers and shareholders is often far from perfect, with management fees linked to company size, incentivising growth but not necessarily profitability, or influencing appraisers. Sometimes it is in the best interests of shareholders to (temporarily) shrink the company by selling assets, for instance, to prepare for a potential downturn, but this is difficult as the manager is not keen to receive smaller fees. Time and again, these businesses start to underperform once the novelty wears off.

There are numerous instances where externally managed vehicles have significantly underperformed benchmark indices for extended periods, resulting in steep valuation discounts to the underlying assets. For example, an EY report cited a 240 basis points underperformance per year for externally managed companies versus internally managed ones in the US real estate investment trust (REIT) market.[1]

This often-persistent underperformance has frequently led to the delisting of the vehicle after a painful period, during which both investors and managers were annoyed with the situation and each other. Shareholders requested changes to the business model, but only marginal adjustments were made. After all, managers are unwilling to give up their lucrative contracts for nothing! In several situations, shareholders ended up paying external managers a significant amount of money to internalise the team. This can be a serious sum: tens of millions or even more than 100 million euros or pounds.

In my experience, externally managed REITs, which are mainly focused on dividend yield, are often poorly structured. Frequently, the payout is not covered by the cash flow after maintenance expenses, the underlying assets are not the best and sometimes the business model is flawed as well. Dramatic examples are social housing providers in the UK, such as Home REIT, where cash flows were far less robust in reality than presented to existing and potential shareholders.

Fortunately, there are now externally managed vehicles available with a higher degree of alignment: lower management fees, share ownership, shorter management contracts, etc. However, it remains crucial to investigate these structures fully, as they are often not clearly explained in presentations or press releases. Don't get stuck as an investor! Occasionally, an externally managed company could be interesting to invest in, but in my view, only if the management has an outstanding long-term track record.

Protection Measures

Some companies implement protection measures such as poison pills or B-shares with fewer voting rights. These measures are intended to block potential hostile takeovers or control opposing shareholders. If the management and board have a proven track record and act sensibly, it may not be a significant issue. However, if these measures are used solely to protect their jobs at the expense of shareholder value, it can be problematic.

Management and Board's Mindset

The mindset of the management and board can vary significantly by jurisdiction, influenced by law and culture. For example, in the US and UK, there is more focus on shareholder value creation, while on the continent, there can be a greater emphasis on long-term value creation **for all stakeholders**, including management, employees, the community, tenants, suppliers and the government. As a result, some companies use this broader focus as an excuse not to act in the interest of shareholders and are often supported by the law in doing so. I have seen many cases where the board or management teams took actions that made them look favourable to other stakeholders but less so to the shareholders. Examples include overspending on environmental, social and governance (ESG) initiatives (with unclear value creation for shareholders), refusing a capital return or takeover bid and incurring high costs (often related to salaries or expensive offices).

Investigate the Shareholder Base

Liquidity of Shares

If the shares are illiquid, it might take time to purchase a position in the company, with the risk of pushing the share price upwards. One might be fortunate to find a block of shares, but liquidity might not be available upon exit and often completely dries up during a downturn. As a result, a liquidity discount should be applied in the underwriting for illiquid stocks. In my view, one should only invest in illiquid stocks if they offer significant upside and tick all the right boxes: assets with strong fundamentals, a strong balance sheet and management that knows what they are doing.

Are Other Shareholders Like-Minded?

A careful due diligence of the shareholder base is required: who are the current investors? Are there any familiar names? In particular:

- **Any large shareholders?** What is their goal? Keep in mind that typically only 50% of the shareholders vote at a shareholders' meeting, so if there is a 25% shareholder, they effectively control 50% of the vote and can significantly influence company policy. Large shareholders can have varying intentions: some may be supportive, while others might depress the share price for a lowball takeover bid later, or control the company for their own purposes, often in ways that are not beneficial (very long-term thinking, reduced transparency, related party transactions, etc.). Be cautious with large, unknown shareholders. I have seen few situations that ended well.
- **What type of investors are in the shareholder base?** Real estate specialists, i.e. investors with funds that only invest in listed real estate stocks, tend to be more long term and supportive than general equity

160   REAL ESTATE RULES

investors, who may follow trends and move to other sectors, or hedge funds, which are even more fickle and may short the stock. Another consideration is whether the existing shareholders run a benchmark fund (as those investors tend to move on more easily without a fight), a private equity fund (which typically has a finite end date and might force an outcome at some point) or an activist fund (which is likely there to shake things up).

Note

1. EY (2017) 'Internal vs. external management structures'.

Chapter 18

Be Aware of Self-Liquidating Companies

I have seen many investors, particularly private investors, buying real estate stocks due to the high dividend yield. Repeatedly, these stocks have underperformed compared to lower-yielding real estate stocks and have often ended up in deep trouble. It follows the same principle as Rule 1: 'High yield for a reason' (discussed in Chapter 1), which often indicates lower-quality assets, a weak growth outlook and other issues. Additionally, these high yields are frequently coupled with a dividend policy that is not sustainable in the long term.

Unsustainable Dividends

It is truly striking how frequently companies set dividends that are unsustainable in the long term. If not properly set, the dividend can be

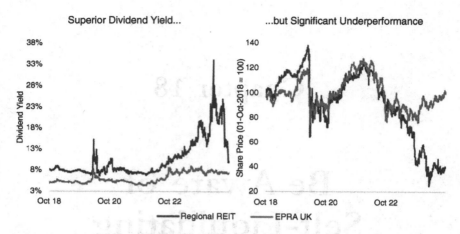

Figure 18.1 Regional REIT – higher dividend yield, lower share price
Note: European Public Real Estate Association (EPRA) UK dividend yield estimated with top five constituents in 2024.
Source: FactSet.

easily reduced or cancelled when adverse market conditions arise, which is poorly received by the equity market. Years of overdistribution, high financial leverage and a deteriorating outlook for real estate create a toxic mix, resulting in companies scrambling for cash by cutting the dividend, reducing capital expenditure (capex) and trying to dispose of properties in a difficult market. The house of cards implodes. These companies end up liquidating themselves, as has been the case for Regional real estate investment trust (REIT) (Figure 18.1).

Sustainable Dividend Policy

Companies and investors should remember that total return (share price change plus dividend) is what matters, not just the dividend. Additionally, a careful check of the key dividend rules is recommended before investing:

1. **Coverage by operating cash flow:** The dividend should be covered by at least the operating cash flow, taking all recurring portfolio capex into account (Quick check: dividend <85% of cash EPS).
2. **Modest leverage:** The balance sheet should not be too highly leveraged, as a potential downturn could immediately pressure the dividend distribution potential (Quick check: loan-to-value (LTV) <35% and net debt to EBITDA <10×).

3. **Resilient dividend policy:** The communicated dividend policy should be robust enough to withstand economic downturns. For instance, if a company states it will always pay a (growing) dividend, it must ensure the current payout is not too high, leaving room for setbacks. Alternatively, it is better to stick to a certain percentage of recurring profit.

It should be noted that the tax-efficient REIT status might not be ideal for a real estate company if it is forced to pay out too much cash in light of its strategy. There have been numerous cases of self-liquidating companies, particularly in the office sector, but the demise of shopping centre landlord intu is one of the most high-profile examples.

intu Properties Plc – In Denial

intu Properties, previously known as Capital Shopping Centres (CSC) and Liberty International, suffered from the classic real estate mistake of taking on too much financial leverage while paying out more in cash to shareholders than the company generated from rental income minus costs and recurring capital expenditure (capex) requirements. In addition, the governance, in my view, was not optimal, with from 2011 a large dominant investor exercising control that was not aligned with a public market mindset, while its debt structure was complicated and flawed. When real estate fundamentals started to deteriorate, it was too late to turn the tide (Figure 18.2).

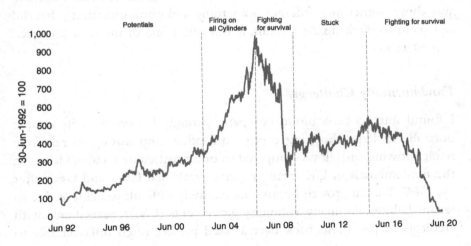

Figure 18.2 intu – turbulent total return story
Source: Adapted from FactSet.

Sir Donald Gordon merged TransAtlantic with the London Stock Exchange (LSE) listed company Capital & Counties in June 1992. The stock price gained 878%, reaching its all-time high in November 2006. That is a compounded return of 17.2% per annum – a stellar performance. Returns were obviously not linear over this period, but the company had a good edge with its focus on high-quality shopping centres in the UK. It was a leader in this segment with ownership of malls at Lakeside (Thurrock), Metrocentre (Gateshead), Braehead (Glasgow) and the Harlequin (Watford). Moreover, it had a second stock listing in Johannesburg (South Africa), where it also had a significant audience.

It is fair to say that intu was on the highway to success. But then the Global Financial Crisis (GFC) came just after intu became a UK REIT on 1 January 2007, which brought the company from the 'firing on all cylinders' phase straight down to 'fighting for survival', after which it moved into the 'stuck' category, only to slide into 'fighting for survival' again. This time, however, it could not be saved.

Although the business was increasingly structurally challenged, it carried on with a 'business as usual' mindset, focusing on acquisition-led growth and believing that its centres would flourish in the long term. By the time intu realised things were worse than expected, it was too late. It was not properly prepared for potential setbacks: financial leverage was too high, cash flow too low and dividend pay-out too high. A deadly combination.

From 2004 onwards, I started looking at intu in closer detail, but there was always something different, something awkward, something that did not seem to stack up. As a result, it was often one of my least preferred real estate stocks.

Fundamentally Challenged

I found intu to be a proud company, strongly believing in its unique portfolio of large shopping centres and often emphasising its relatively stable growing cash flows compared to other real estate sectors. However, the fundamentals in UK retail property weakened faster and faster after the GFC. Rental growth became increasingly difficult to achieve due to tenant failures, company voluntary agreements (CVAs: agreements with creditors to pay them back over a fixed period, often unfavourable to landlords), weak consumer spending, ecommerce eating into store sales and higher costs for retailers (e.g. driven by a weak pound or increased minimum wages).

In addition, landlords of UK shopping centres generally have limited insight into turnover data of tenants, making it difficult to assess how well tenants are trading, what needs to be changed and what rent they can demand. Where turnover statistics were available, there were cases where retailers deducted returns of internet purchases from the revenue, which was also unhelpful. Another problem was the business rates. These are, in my eyes, ridiculous taxes paid by the tenants, typically around 30–40% of the rent. Nevertheless, if a unit becomes vacant and is not let within three months, the landlord must pay this tax! As such, the landlord could end up with no rent, costs of the vacant unit and a tax on top of that! Disaster. This is why there are often charity shops in retail units. Typically, they pay a modest rent and sometimes even nothing, but at least the landlord does not incur the costs and the business rates. All of this was obviously made even worse by Brexit and later COVID, when malls were forced to close, and it was legal for tenants not to pay rent during this period. It was astonishing that several healthy trading retailers withheld rental payments to mall owners during COVID, adding to the landlord's agony.

intu was working hard to maintain its occupancy, although it was increasingly difficult, as many retailers were struggling, while there was too much retail space in the UK and so many shops to fill in a centre (typically more than 200). In my view, some centres had just become too big over the years through extensions. There were simply not enough healthy tenants competing for these units to create price tension. As a result, shopping centres started to attract other types of retail such as food and beverage, but rents were lower compared to the departing fashion retailers. Unfortunately, many would also go into administration years later.

All of this hit intu's like-for-like rental growth, which was close to an average of 6% in the four years before the GFC, but fell to an average of −1% in the years after that. In addition, intu had to spend increasingly significant amounts on its malls to keep them attractive for tenants and shoppers. Working hard but still steadily moving backwards. Whilst shopping centre valuations rebounded after the GFC, this was driven by financial stimulus. However, the weight of worsening fundamentals increasingly got the upper hand. Whereas intu's mall values rose by 17.4% between 2004 and 2006, they would subsequently fall by 42.9% by the end of 2019, the last reported valuation by the company (Figure 18.3). As I estimate that values would have fallen by another 25–30% in 2020, the total drop from the peak would have been around 60%, indicating the book equity was most likely gone.

In Denial

So, the mall fundamentals were awful in those years, worse than anybody could have imagined. However, I do believe intu suffered from what Andrew Jones tends to call the Stockholm syndrome for real estate. The board was in love with its malls and downplaying the structural threats. Frequently, the poor retailer results were blamed on the weather or fewer trading days in the month compared to the previous year. Fine, this can be the case, but not consistently. Also, the largest shareholder, the impressive billionaire John Whittaker, who kept increasing his stake in the company over the years from 23.2% in 2011 on a diluted basis to 27.32% in 2019, always stressed thinking long term. In my view, this approach overlooked short-term challenges and encouraged further

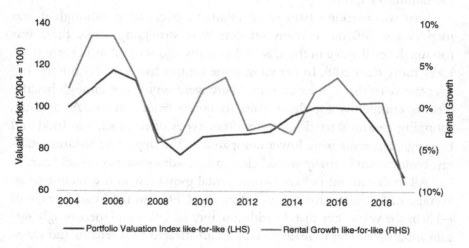

Figure 18.3 intu – the road of decline: lower rental growth, falling values
Source: intu annual reports.

acquisition-led growth. I found it dangerous, as I have seen this way of thinking with other successful investors in the direct property market, but times were changing faster and faster, and the listed market works differently than the direct market, which is repeatedly overlooked.

Although the tone in later annual reports was not as bullish as in the earlier years, it remained very positive, even if, in my view, key data were harder to find, as a lot of marketing nonsense was added to the reports: the malls will be just fine in the long term. What's more, while it claimed in its 2014 annual report that it had always been at the forefront of technology, that was never my impression as an analyst. I have studied all the annual reports and did not read much, if anything, about the internet, online, Amazon or ecommerce until the report of 2012, which was published in 2013. It contained a full campaign, including rebranding to intu from CSC, the launch of an internet site, free Wi-Fi and service centres in the malls. But in 2012, the internet penetration was already 10% in the UK. I remember the rebranding to intu in 2013 very well. We, the JP Morgan research team, offered a couple of explanations for what intu stood for. One of them made it into the press: 'Improving Nothing, Terminal Underperformer'. Sadly, that is what happened.

I was generally satisfied with the reporting and transparency of the company, as many metrics were consistently reported in the same way, and details per shopping centre were disclosed. There was one thing, though, that I and other analysts were not happy with. When problems started because of the GFC, new lettings were done at 20% below the last passing rent in 2009, while nearly half of the new leases were short term and 35% lower. In the subsequent years, the company only reported the uplifts on *long-term* lettings, while the percentage of *short-term* leases with significant discounts grew in the industry.

The worsening fundamentals, a board in denial and a feeling that things were worse beneath the data increasingly resulted in tension at analyst meetings. I recall leading investor Marcus Phayre-Mudge, manager of TR Property Investment Trust since 2011 and partner at Thames River Capital, now part of Columbia Threadneedle Investments, asking a crucial question at one of these meetings, which was rebuffed by the CEO with: 'What a daft question!' The audience was flabbergasted.

Even the Sky Is Not the Limit

But the saga that kicked off at the end of 2010 would become one of my most memorable. It said a lot about the board and its blue-sky thinking and would always be a reminder to me in the back of my mind. It started with intu, at that time called Capital Shopping Centres (CSC), proposing to buy the Trafford Centre in Manchester from Peel Group, founded by John Whittaker, in exchange for shares priced at 368p per share. After completion, Peel Group would hold a fully diluted ownership of 24.7% in CSC. The intrinsic value (net asset value (NAV)) of intu was at that time 390p per share (year-end actual 2010), so the shares would be issued to Peel at a 5.6% discount. The acquisition of the Trafford Centre would make CSC the leading shopping centre group in Britain, with four out of the top six out-of-town shopping centres and 10 out of the top 25 malls.

However, the US retail property giant Simon Property, which owned more than 5% of CSC at the time, arrived on the scene with some fireworks. It said that intu shareholders would be foolish to accept this deal as they would hand over control to Peel at too low a price. A battle had begun. After several strong public interactions between Simon and CSC, the US giant proposed the board with an indicative offer subject to due diligence for the company of 425p per share in mid-December 2010. CSC countered that the bid undervalued the company with its 'irreplaceable and unrivalled portfolio'. Simon's pressure did, however, result in a proposal to increase the price for the shares to be issued to Peel from 368p to 400p, which would reduce its ownership in CSC to 23.2% from 24.7% on a fully diluted basis.

Because of all the turmoil, the Extraordinary General Meeting (EGM) to vote on the Peel transaction was rescheduled from 20 December 2010 to 26 January 2011. Simon withdrew its bid on 11 January, because, I believe, it recognised it would be hard to win the battle. Nevertheless, CSC's board was now in full fighting mode. It published a report before the EGM in which it concluded that the company was potentially worth 625p per share (!!!) and that Simon 'substantially undervalued the company'. This valuation would imply a premium of 60% to the 2010 NAV of 390p. Wow! It was a highly remarkable report (see Figure 18.4). I kept a copy in one of my boxes over the years, as I believed it was a collector's item – it is! I could not agree more with Simon at the time, who commented that this valuation was full of 'wishful thinking'.

Be Aware of Self-Liquidating Companies

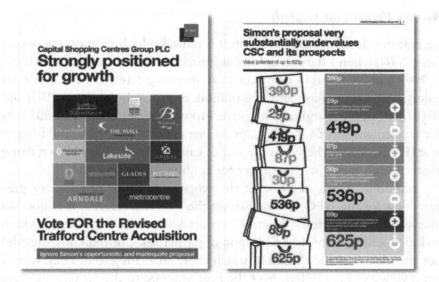

Figure 18.4 CSC's (intu's) defence document

The report estimated a fair value potential from 390p per share to 625p, with the main drivers coming from 'Independent assessment of additional value realisable through a disposal of the portfolio as a whole today' (+89p), 'Adjusting property values to mid-point in the cycle' (+87p), 'Development opportunities' (+30p) and 'Reversal of Stamp Duty Land Tax deduction' (+29p). All these points had yet to be proven over time.

The whole report read like an election brochure, which included a banner at the bottom of every left page: 'Ignore Simon's opportunistic and inadequate proposal' and on the right page: 'Vote FOR Revised Trafford Centre Acquisition'. In the end, 82% of shareholders voted in favour of the Peel Group transaction, with strong support from the South African shareholder base.

The company was now in the 'stuck' phase. It remained convinced about the power of large shopping centres and continued its acquisition-led growth, ignoring the worsening fundamentals and failing to prepare for setbacks. The share price would never again rise above 400p. Worse, it was on a slippery declining slope, heading to the phase of 'fighting for survival'. intu did not, or did not want to see it, but many did. Indeed, the Stockholm syndrome for real estate.

Always Focused on Growth

Against this deteriorating backdrop, it is remarkable that almost every year since 2004, when I started looking at intu, it has been a net investor. Only in 2004 and 2019 was its cash flow from investing positive (i.e. it was a net seller), with £85 million and £76 million, respectively, whilst in 2010 and 2018, it was only marginally negative. However, from 2005 until 2017, its net investment was £4.4 billion, or an average of almost £340 million per year (Figure 18.5). There was no year of caution. The belief was that being bigger meant more pricing power for landlords over retailers.

Although it was not one of the worst companies in terms of preparedness for the GFC, it was also not the best and surely not as good as they claimed in their 2008 annual report with their 'early steps', which included selling more than £1 billion of properties. Conveniently, they did not mention that they invested much more than they sold. They were a net investor of £2.1 billion over the four years up to the GFC!

Over the years, it developed and extended shopping centres in the UK, had exposure to the US, held a stake in an Indian developer and was happily building a portfolio in Spain with acquisitions of Parque Principado in Asturias (2013), Puerto Venecia in Zaragoza (2015) and Xanadu shopping centre in Madrid (2017) at a time when it found itself increasingly on the downward spiral of doom. Quite astonishing. Besides sailing close to the wind in terms of financial leverage, it also booked acquisition-related expenses through the profit and loss account over the years 2010–2018, which added up to a total of £95 million. I did not understand why these

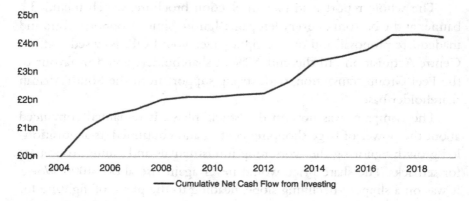

Figure 18.5 intu – a net investor
Source: intu annual reports.

costs were reported as exceptional administration expenses, as they appeared every year of these nine years. That is not exceptional. That is regular.

Whilst the company was highly focused on growth (the title of its 2010 annual report was: 'Strongly positioned for growth'), I did applaud them for the demerger carried out in May 2010, when Capital & Counties (Capco), which owned Covent Garden and a large residential development site in London, was spun out of the company. I loved Capco: a clean company, strong management, an attractive investment story and valuation. What I especially liked: management was able to present the investment case in a minute with clear ballpark numbers. I remained Underweight on intu, though. It looked expensive and not dynamic.

Too Close to the Wind

The company did finance part of its purchases with the issuance of fresh equity. Over the period 2004–2019, it issued net cash equity (also taking into account share purchases and sales) of £2.27 billion. The problem was the net debt pile expanded by £2.94 billion up to 2018 (almost £700 million more), after which it declined by £369 million in 2019, but that was still a growth of 5.5% p.a. over 16 years. Over the years, the amount of net debt was on average equal to its market capitalisation (although this was not the case from 2016 anymore, when net debt was significantly higher), its LTV ratio around 50% and its net debt-to-EBITDA ratio most of the time above 10 times. This was pushing the boundaries in terms of financial leverage (Figure 18.6).

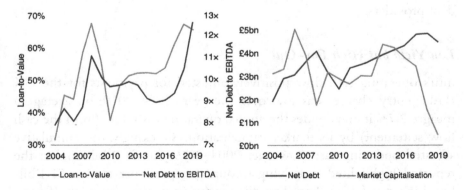

Figure 18.6 Leverage too high and mountain of debt breaks company
Source: FactSet; intu annual reports.

172   REAL ESTATE RULES

In intu's case, the LTV should be significantly below 40% and net debt to EBITDA significantly below 10 times. In 2004, the leverage was actually in balance: market capitalisation of £3.1 billion, net debt of £1.9 billion, LTV ratio of 36% and net debt to EBITDA of 7.3 times, but that was not the case in later years. The high financial leverage resulted in significant shareholder value destruction when the GFC hit and when its business was highly challenged in 2018–2020. Both times, it was caught out by financial markets. The fact that the company had borrowings secured against assets, but those vehicles had lent money to the parent, resulted in a complicated structure with numerous misaligned creditors, accelerating its eventual downfall.

Things were bad during the GFC. The opening comment of intu's chairman in the 2008 annual report says it all:

> 2008 has been a year that the UK property industry would like to forget, but no doubt its unremitting gloom will be long remembered. In the last quarter, an already uncertain market dropped further following the crisis in the banking sector. While Liberty International's high-quality assets are resilient, with prime regional shopping centres amounting to 70% of the total and retail property 85% overall, we are not immune to market stresses.

In 2009, it issued equity twice: in May for net proceeds of £592 million and in October for £274 million, resulting in a total of £866 million. Although the terms were not as dilutive as some of the other listed REITs, the issuances did dilute EPS by 25.9% and the NAV per share by 22.1%. However, acting late proved disastrous in 2018–2020. No help was available, no buyers for its assets, no takers of new equity and no lenient debt providers.

Low Yield but High Pay-Out

intu's operating cash flow, positively adjusted for payments for the UK REIT entry charge, was low over the years 2004–2019: on average a meagre 2.7% if one divides the annual operating cash flow (from the cash flow statement) by its market capitalisation. Shockingly, the cumulative adjusted operating cash flow over 2004–2019 was £1.2 billion, but the reported/highlighted underlying accountancy profit pre-tax was £1.1 billion higher at £2.3 billion. The difference was mainly the result of non-cash items in the underlying profit, e.g. related to tenant incentives and capitalised interest, and the exclusion of extraordinary costs, which in reality were quite regular. Interestingly, almost every year over the analysed period the company saw an increase in its balance sheet item 'trade & other receivables', which means that tenants owed the company more and more. However, this was increasingly difficult to collect.

Despite this cash-mismatch, intu was paying out generous cash dividends, which were not covered by the adjusted operating cash flow. Over the period 2004–2019 about £500 million was paid out in cash dividends that were not covered by cash flow. If one also assumes that these centres would need additional capex to remain up to date, which is not provided for in the operating cash flow, then, assuming an average provision of 10% of net rental income for capex, the surplus payout was as high as £1.1 billion (Figure 18.7). If the shareholders had always opted for a cash dividend (the company offered a scrip dividend from 2012 onwards), the surplus would have been another £200 million higher. High financial leverage and a too high cash dividend payout always ends badly when times take a turn for the worse. If this happens, a company attempts to de-leverage every possible way, starting with reducing costs and followed by a dividend cut if that is not enough. Repeatedly, it does not stop there and an emergency equity raising is needed – often on disastrous terms – and when that is no longer possible only praying for a miraculous survival is left. In intu's case, it was the end. Green Street nicely summarised its downfall: 'intu's

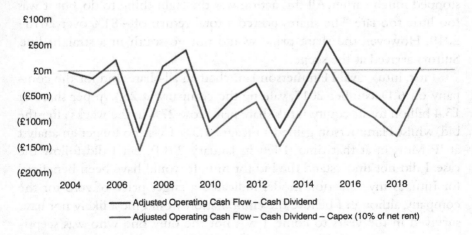

Figure 18.7 intu – paying out too much cash dividend almost every year
Source: Author estimates based on intu annual reports.

174

REAL ESTATE RULES

pains appear to be largely self-inflicted; management appear to hope for the best, rather than preparing for the worst'.

The End

intu's business went from 'running hard to stand still' to 'running as fast as you can on an escalator that moves at full speed in the opposite direction'. The years 2018, and especially 2019 and 2020, were very painful. Like-for-like rental growth was a marginal 0.6% in 2018 and a whopping −9.1% in 2019, heavily impacted by vacancy, administrations and CVAs. Excluding the impact of capital investment, the numbers were even lower, +0.4% and −10.3%, respectively. The shopping centre valuations plummeted by 32.6% over these two years, resulting in a 60% hit on NAV and a jump in the LTV ratio to 67.8% − way too high for comfort for all stakeholders. Although the company was not a net investor in 2018 and 2019 (for a change), it was also unable to generate significant amounts of cash. The net cash flow from investing was £0m in 2018 and only +£76 million in 2019, when it managed to dispose of part of the mall in Derby for £186 million. It also sold the centres Puerto Venecia (£201 million) and Asturias (£123m), but these transactions would close in 2020 and bring the 2019 pro-forma LTV a bit down to 65.3%. In addition, it reduced overhead costs by 10% in 2019 and did not pay a cash dividend in that year, which should have obviously been reduced or stopped much earlier. All this action was the right thing to do, but it was too little too late. The shares posted a total return of −81% over 2018–2019. However, the share price would not go south in a straight line. Suitors arrived at the scene.

First, intu's rival Hammerson launched an all-shares bid for the company on 6 December 2017, valuing the company at 253.9p per share or £3.4 billion for its equity. intu's share price rose 27% in the weeks after the bid, whilst Hammerson gained a meagre 1.5%. I was no longer an analyst at JP Morgan at that time (I left in January 2014), but I did follow the case. I did not understand the bid for intu. It would have been beneficial for Intu, as my valuation model indicated a target price of zero for the company, although I believe the combination would most likely not have survived in the years to come. I was not the only one who was sceptical, as Hammerson's share price soon started a sharp decline, losing 17% in 2.5 months. Continental European rival Klépierre, backed by its large shareholder Simon Property (which held more than 20% of the shares in Klépierre), was quick to react and approached the board of Hammerson with a non-binding proposal to acquire the company on 19 March 2018, valuing its equity at £4.9 billion. Hammerson's share price bounced 24%. I thought it was a classic Simon move – acting on the vulnerability of Hammerson and frustrating its bid for intu, leaving the latter potentially struggling for survival. However, Hammerson's board was quick to dismiss the proposal and also the revised 3% higher offer, after which Klépierre walked away. In the meantime, the UK retail (property) market continued to worsen, and many investors had sounded their concerns to Hammerson about its bid for intu. Hammerson's board had carefully listened and withdrew its recommendation to vote in favour of the acquisition on 18 April 2018. Its shareholders voted one week later against the combination. Many investors breathed a sigh of relief, although there was also disappointment in the board's handling of the intu situation and probably even more in the rejection of the Klépierre proposal. Hammerson's shares would return −83% from 25 April 2018 till the end of 2020.

On 4 October 2018, the largest intu shareholder Peel Group, together with Olyan Group and Brookfield Property Group, arrived on the scene considering a possible offer of 215p per share, valuing the equity at £2.9 billion. intu's share price jumped 27.2%. But after several extensions of the deadline to finalise their takeover offer, they decided not to bid for intu at the end of November, which in my view was the result of poor prospects for UK retail property and concerns from Brookfield shareholders. In 2019, intu was in free fall, with the shares generating a total return of −70%. Its 2019 annual report said:

> In the short term, fixing the balance sheet is our top priority. The notes accompanying these financial statements indicate a *material uncertainty in relation to intu's ability to continue as a going concern*. However, we have options including alternative capital structures and further disposals to provide liquidity, and will seek to negotiate covenant waivers where appropriate. These would address potential covenant remedies and the upcoming refinancing activities, with the first material debt maturities in early 2021. (emphasis added)

At the start of 2020, the company sounded out investors for their appetite for raising £1.3 billion in new equity, very close to what they had overpaid in dividends between 2004 and 2018. In March,

176   REAL ESTATE RULES

intu concluded there was no support, which was not surprising. Then
COVID hit. It was the final nail in the coffin. I believe it would have
fallen over anyway, but the pandemic did speed up intu's downfall. In
April/May restructuring lawyers were instructed, and KPMG were
appointed as administrators in June 2020. On 26 June 2020, intu fell
into administration, according to the press because pension fund CPPIB
did not agree with debt amendments and seized control of the Trafford
Centre. A long process of sorting out the mess started with nothing left
for equity holders. The company had liquidated itself.

Chapter 19

When Trust Is Gone, There Is No Limit to Downside

The equity market does not like uncertainty and definitely not lost trust. It operates on the principle: 'If in doubt, throw it out'. This means that if you have doubts about the investment case, the intentions of a company, or what is the truth, just sell the shares! Don't convince yourself it will be okay. The equity market always heavily discounts uncertainty and there is no limit to the downside in the event of a complete loss of trust. Once trust is gone, it is extremely hard to rebuild it.

Spotting Red Flags

It is important to spot the red flags that can put companies into serious trouble and result in a significant loss of trust from the capital markets. Investors should conduct careful due diligence. One does not want to regret the investment one day.

177

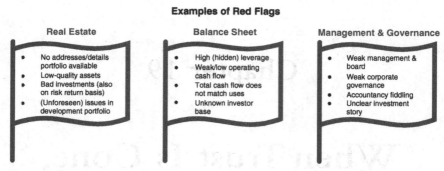

Source: Author.

Investors need to ensure that the real estate portfolio can deliver the expected returns, the balance sheet is secure in every unforeseen situation and that the management and board act in the best interest of shareholders. It is a red flag if companies do not communicate the addresses of the properties in the portfolio. It is a red flag when there is limited operating cash flow in the company compared to the reported accountancy earnings (how can the dividend be paid?) or when a company commits to large investments in the future without having the financing in place (capital markets are not always open at the same terms). It is a red flag when the management is weak, e.g. ill-defined strategy, poor execution, poor track record, poor communication (not telling the full truth), or when corporate governance is weak, e.g. poor accountability (including accounting tricks), alignment (including related party transactions) and transparency.

In the most recent downturn, there were two companies that stood out in this category: SBB and Adler Group.

The Downfall of SBB

SBB, with its impossible name Samhällsbyggnadsbolaget i Norden AB, is a Swedish real estate company founded in 2016. It is involved in the development and management of social infrastructure properties, which include schools, healthcare facilities, municipal buildings, and residential properties. SBB's history has been marked by aggressive expansion fuelled by cheap debt, quintupling its portfolio and pushing its share price up by over 500% since 2017 to a peak in December 2021 (Figure 19.1). Its shares soared 141% from the beginning of 2021 to their high in November alone (!!), but subsequently crashed in 2022/23, falling more

When Trust Is Gone, There Is No Limit to Downside

Figure 19.1 SBB versus European Public Real Estate Association (EPRA) Sweden and EPRA Europe – total return
Source: Adapted from FactSet.

than 95% (!!), as the complexity and scale of its debt became problematic when interest rates started to rise, the economic environment turned more challenging, and major governance concerns were exposed.

In 2022, critical reports from short sellers highlighted SBB's opaque accounting, poor governance and excessive leverage. These reports specifically accused SBB of engaging in round-tripping by using its preferred equity SBB-D shares as incentives in property deals with owner-operators. SBB would buy properties from owner-operators, paying partly with SBB-D shares (associated with high dividends), allowing the operator to pay higher rents and SBB to show higher valuations in the books. Furthermore, transactions with apparent related parties were not transparently reported, as they served the purpose of proving book values.

Additionally, governance was compromised by a dual-class share structure allowing management to control over 50% of the voting rights with just a 15% equity stake. The board composition also raised further concerns about governance, as it seemed not to be as independent as portrayed.

From 2022 to 2024, SBB severely struggled under its complicated debt pile and resulting credit rating downgrades. Rating agency S&P wrote in March 2024: 'SBB's capital structure remains unsustainable based on continued weak liquidity with significant short-term debt maturities'. It had a 'junk bond' (also called speculative) issue rating varying between

D (Default) and CCC (three notches above D, but three notches below investment grade) in the first part of 2024. On top of that, some debt holders claimed that the company had violated covenants demanding immediate repayment, which the company vigorously refuted.

As a result, SBB was in significant deleveraging mode, which included strategic disposals, debt restructuring, issuance of preference shares and the pausing of payments on its hybrid bonds to handle upcoming debt maturities. Additionally, SBB split the group into three units: – community, education and residential – with the aim of selling parts of these businesses, including IPOs, as was the case with the residential platform Neobo Fastigheter and Sveafastigheter. The Swedish Financial Supervisory Authority also started an investigation to determine if there had been any breaches of accounting rules. All of this could not, of course, be executed by the current management, which was replaced. Besides, the board was overhauled.

The SBB investment story was completely destroyed. It was uninvestable: too complicated, too speculative. As a result, the daily volatility, a measure of uncertainty, of the SBB shares shot through the roof, with an average absolute daily share price change of 5% over the period from May 2023 to May 2024 versus 2% over the period before from 2021 to 2022 (Figure 19.2). On 30 October 2023, the share price hit an all-time low of 2.96 SEK (down 95% since its 2021 peak). SBB kept struggling in 2024 facing debt maturities of $1.8 billion (SEK 18 billion) in 2024 and 2025.

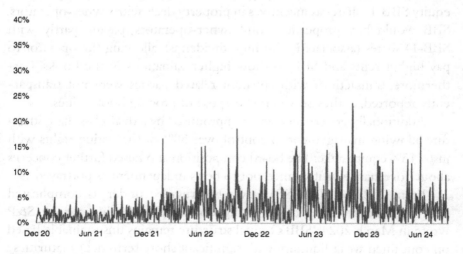

Figure 19.2 SBB daily share price volatility
Source: Data from FactSet.

Adler Group: Everything That Possibly Could Go Wrong Went Wrong

Lots of Drama

The story of Adler Group S.A. ('Adler') is a bizarre one. It is full of drama, bad corporate governance and unexpected twists. It is a case of how not to do things. A case of complete shareholder value destruction. When the company got onto the sliding spiral, it did try to claw back, but the gravity was too strong. Everything that could go wrong went wrong. So many bizarre, unexpected events. Each time when it looked like this was surely it, it could not go any worse, something else (unexpected) would happen and the stock would drop even lower. And lower. It all ended in a vicious downward cycle. The cycle of doom. I had seen many collapses in real estate, but never experienced something like Adler from the front seat.

Warning Signals

At the end of June 2021, the company owned almost 70,000 residential units in Germany with its largest exposure to Berlin (42%), Düsseldorf (10%), Stuttgart (7%) and Hamburg (6%). The total portfolio value amounted to €12.6 billion, of which €3.7 billion was in development. However, there were numerous red flags, especially on cash flow and relatively high financial leverage, and the number of warning signs grew over time. This should have killed the investment story straight away. But not for me. I advised investing in the stock, on the basis that the German residential market was strong, the stock heavily discounted and management showed a willingness to turn the business around. I would be proven wrong in due course, but a wise lesson richer.

Kicking Off

It all started to accelerate at the end of August 2021, when Adler reported at first sight positive half-year results, where full-year guidance was upgraded, with increased disclosure on developments and receivables. Although the company reported a high loan-to-value (LTV) ratio of 54.7%, which would have been above 60% if the receivables/financial assets had not been deducted from net debt, Adler was convinced those receivables would be collected soon (see Figure 19.3 for the key slide of their half-year 2021 results presentation). Besides, the underlying property markets were strong anyway. It looked as though the company was listening and making an effort. The share price went up that day by 5% to €22.50, valuing the shareholders' equity at €2.6 billion. However, we would never see this value again.

The next day the stock declined by 4%. The market was not convinced Adler had financial leverage under control. Interestingly, though, co-CEO Maximilian Rienecker bought 9,500 shares following the results announcement at an average price of €21.39 per share and a total investment of approximately €200,000. Normally, insider trading is a positive signal for the stock, but not this time. It only seemed to make the stock weaker. I started to think that this purchase maybe unintentionally signalled there was no takeover pending or other positive news, as management would otherwise not have been allowed to trade.

The share price movements became increasingly violent, especially at the end of September, when the stock plummeted some days by 5–7% a day! This was not normal. There was something else we did not know. Something must be seriously wrong.

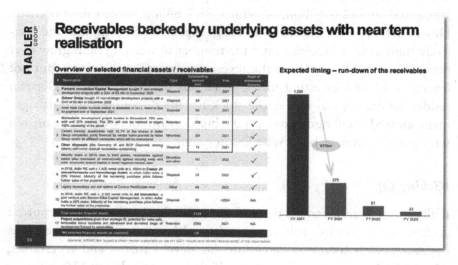

Figure 19.3 Key slide from Adler's half-year 2021 results presentation
Source: Adler Group first half 2021 presentation.

Going to Berlin

We decided to take the plane to Adler's headquarters in Berlin to look the Adler people in the eyes. This did not smell right. I came up with three possible scenarios: (a) there is some kind of fraud or something we do not see; (b) it is related to its large shareholder Aggregate, which had a margin loan on its Adler shares; and (c) its developments are overstated. Unfortunately, our fears would become true.

At Adler's Headquarters

On 6 October 2021, my colleague Luke Green and I were at Adler's headquarters in Berlin. It would be a day we will never forget. At one moment, during a short break in the hallway, we discussed the violent share price moves with the investor relations (IR) officer. Right at that time, a short seller report on Adler Group was published. The IR officer and other Adler employees turned completely pale. Later that day, we visited some properties and development sites in Berlin, but at the (expensive) €226 million Wilhelm project (cost per square metre of circa €14,000) close to the American Embassy, there was not much action – there was only one bulldozer active.

Source: Author.

Which Eagle?

I spoke to a senior person regarding Adler ('eagle' in German) in those days, and he said he could not get used to the Adler Group logo. In his view, the eagle had too much resemblance to the eagle of the Third Reich. He understood that management was fond of the cars of the German Adler brand (German lieutenants drove these cars), and the Adler car company had evolved into Adler Real Estate, but the logo made him uncomfortable. I had not yet noticed the resemblance, but I was earlier astonished and disappointed that the new combination of the three-way merger was called Adler. A weird choice, as Adler Real Estate did not have the best reputation, whereas Ado Properties had. It would have been much better to have taken the name of Ado Properties.

Logo of Adler Group	Logo of Adler automobile company	Logo of Nazi Germany

Source: The original uploader/wilimedia commons/public domain.

The Allegations

The short seller report published by Viceroy made the following allegations. Firstly, that Adler was controlled by an 'undisclosed cabal of kleptocrats' headed by the well-known real estate investor Caner with 'his clan of people' who stole from Adler shareholders by looting the company. It described practices where properties were sold at low prices to related partners, including Caner's family, or at inflated book values to related parties so that the value of the company increased and Adler could take on more debt. The buyer of these assets would typically not pay the full price (the remainder would be recorded as a receivable by Adler), but the title would be transferred to the buyer who would then borrow against the asset to pay Adler a part of the purchase price without putting equity itself into the transaction. This also gave some optional value to the buyer as he could potentially 'flip' it later to somebody for a higher price and, if not, return it to Adler. Astonishing practices. Secondly, it argued that the value of the development portfolio was overstated with many projects being delayed. Thirdly, it argued that the yielding portfolio was overvalued in the books as well, but I did not agree with this allegation. In my view, this third argument was added to topple the company, as, if this was true, the company would surely be in default. Property prices would indeed start to decline in 2022, but this was the result of a sudden increase in interest rates, which would bring the company completely to its knees.

KPMG Investigation

Adler announced an independent investigation into the transactions and valuation process, to be executed by KPMG, but they were also the auditor, albeit a different team. This was a major mistake. One should not hire the statutory auditor as a forensic investigator as well, due to the inherent conflict of interest and the potential for resulting delays in obtaining conclusive results.

It took a long time for the KPMG forensic team to publish the report – much longer than expected and what was guided for by the company. Its 2021 full-year results release had to be postponed. Eventually, the KPMG report was published in April 2022. It mentioned many things that looked suspicious or were just wrong. In my view, it is clear that there was limited due diligence carried out on major transactions, there were numerous related party transactions, corporate governance was weak to say the least, the development business was a mess and there were accounting irregularities, e.g. regarding the Gerresheim development project. For me, an exemplary example was that management had also bought bonds issued by Aggregate, its largest shareholder, as they thought they were good value (!). That is not right and shows, in my view, how interconnected these companies operated. KPMG stated frequently in the report that they did not have access to all emails or information in general and that Adler was slow to respond to their requests.

After the release, the KPMG auditor issued a disclaimer of opinion for the consolidated financial statements and the annual accounts 2021, which means the accounts were audited but not 'fully' approved. Soon, KPMG would quit as an auditor, and it would take a long time for Adler to find a new one. Adler was firmly on a vicious downward spiral filled with bizarre events, which was accelerated by a declining property market (Figure 19.4).

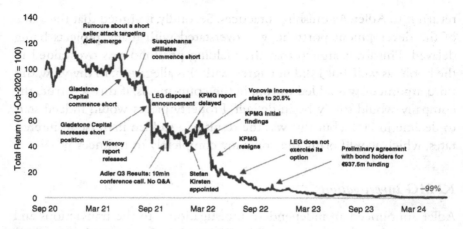

Figure 19.4 Adler Group – everything went wrong
Source: FactSet; Adler Group press releases; BaFin.

The Perfect Short Seller Attack

The short sellers played their game really well. It was a masterclass. Many short sellers were involved. It was well coordinated. They shorted the equity, shorted the bonds, shorted financial instruments of subsidiaries and shorted the debt of the largest shareholder. And with so much force that these prices collapsed, triggering margin calls from certain investors, which forced them to sell as well. For example, Adler issued in January 2021 a €700 million five-year bond with a coupon of 1.875% and an €800 million eight-year bond with a coupon of 2.25%. Now the (implied) yield of these (and other Adler) bonds was skyrocketing, resulting in lower bond prices, i.e. losses (Figure 19.5).

The short sellers were continuously attacking and accusing the company of severe wrongdoing in almost every area. They accused it of fraud, put it in the same category as Wirecard (one of the biggest fraud scandals ever), called it uninvestable and made a lot of noise: in the press, with analysts, on X (with bomb explosions) and on any kind of (investor) forum, including suggestive questions on conference calls. They sent letters to regulators. They just did not let go. Once short sellers attack, they not only come in large numbers but also don't let go easily. It was a coordinated, relentless attack to seed so much doubt with the goal that trust from the investment community would be lost, lost forever. Lost trust that would result in financial default and potentially destroy the company. The ultimate goal of short sellers is to make as much money as possible.

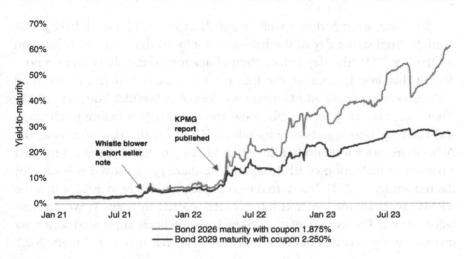

Figure 19.5 Adler Group – bond yields rising sharply
Source: FactSet; Adler Group press releases.

What's more, Adler was attacked on so many fronts, so severely and with such detail, that it would take time for Adler to respond. Its defence would have to be factual, strong and convincing. No doubt could remain because short sellers will attack you on that. Again, financial markets do not like doubt. They give big discounts for that. As a result, Adler had to hire a third party (KPMG) to carry out an independent investigation, which was going to take significant time. All this time, the accusations were 'hanging' above the company, seeding unrest.

The combination of shorting all financial instruments with force and the subsequent collapse in prices, the continuous flow of accusations and Adler's long time to respond, made Adler uninvestable. The situation became so complex that 'normal' investors (let alone retail investors!) would need a day job just to keep up to speed. And not only equity investors, but also bond investors and other third parties. This increasingly choked off access to any kind of capital and damaged relationships with other stakeholders, such as suppliers who wanted to get paid, employees whose careers were being damaged, municipalities who didn't want to be involved as well as appraisers and auditors, none of whom wanted a claim against them; all these factors cumulatively damaging the business beyond repair. No access to financing could potentially result in financial default or an expensive restructuring of liabilities, exactly what eventually happened.

So, things went perfectly well for the short sellers. The stock fell by 40% from 31 August, the day of the half-year results, to the close of business on 5 October 2021, the day before the publication of the short seller report. To put this drop in context: the European real estate benchmark returned −8% over this period and German residential bellwether Vonovia −9.1%. There were clearly people who knew about this report before publication and built up positions before its release. Then on the day of release, the Adler share price lost another 26%, plummeting to €10 per share, implying a market capitalisation of €1.2 billion. The share price moved sideways for the remainder of 2021, but started to collapse completely in 2022 when the KPMG report came out and interest rates started to jump. It would have fallen over if Professor Stefan Kirsten had not been appointed as a new member of the board of directors and elected as chairman in February 2022.

'I'm still standing'

I know Kirsten from my time at JP Morgan, as I was the sell–side analyst involved with the marketing of the Deutsche Annington IPO, which later evolved into Vonovia. He was the chief financial officer (CFO). A strong personality. A bit arrogant, but he knows his stuff for sure. I like him. Often smoking a big cigar after the dinners we had.

Kirsten was passionate about reviving Adler: trust needed to be restored. He was right in saying about the short sellers: 'They picked indeed the weakest sheep of the pack. . .'. As a token of his conviction, he bought shares four times for a total of approximately €1.5 million, on which he would suffer significant losses. He was not liked by the short sellers and maybe he should have handled certain situations differently, but he did save the company multiple times, e.g. by publishing results on the last day possible or by pushing through the restructuring plan at the end of 2022. He would say to me: 'A cat has nine lives; we have more than three'. Or when I called him once, he answered singing: 'I'm still standing. . .'. He was the right person Adler needed ('I like this stuff, I am like a pig in the mud, I love it'), but only much earlier. Unfortunately, Kirsten had to quit the board in February 2024 due to health reasons. As of writing (end 2024), Adler is still standing, but only just. It finally published its audited 2022 and 2023 annual reports with unqualified audit opinions on 30 September 2024, indicating no significant issues with the financial statements for these years.

My advice on Adler Group was not my finest moment. However, we cut our losses early. In my experience, when short sellers launch a full-scale attack and their case is compelling, the stock tends to underperform for an extended period. In such situations, shareholders should act swiftly: accept the loss, sell and move on, as it often goes from bad to worse as we saw with Adler (Figure 19.6).

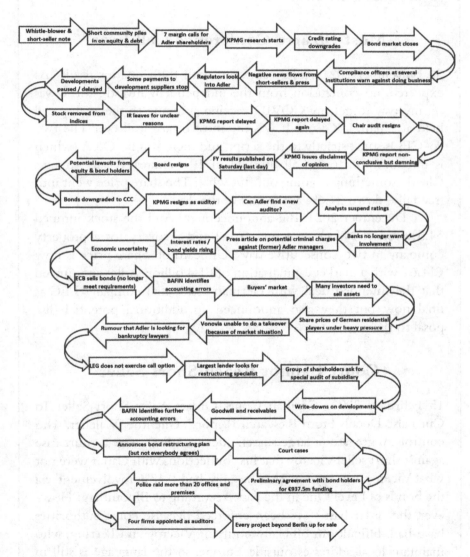

Figure 19.6 Adler Group's vicious downward spiral
Note: ECB (European Central Bank). LEG (LEG Immobilien; a German residential property company). BAFIN (the Federal Financial Supervisory Authority in Germany).
Source: Author; Adler Group.

Adler Group: So Many Bizarre Events

I started to keep a diary during the Adler saga. Below are passages about some bizarre events.

Most Bizarre Conference Call Ever

30 November 2021. Adler came out with third-quarter results. As expected, no conclusion from the independent investigator. I was on my way to get my COVID vaccine, listening to the analyst call held at 2 p.m. UK time. It was the most bizarre call ever. The two co-CEOs stuck strictly to the script, and there was no Q&A (which is uncommon). It was all finished in 10 minutes. Really strange. Clearly something is going on! But what? The share price went into free fall – down 21.6% at the end of the day.

1 December 2021. Big announcement! And the stock jumped 34.5% today! Never seen such a fall and recovery for a property company in two consecutive days! Unheard of! Share price is now €11.61 with a market capitalisation of €1.4 billion. Adler announced that the intended deal with German residential company LEG is final now, but they also announced an additional potential disposal to them.

Court Cannot Reach Short Seller

15 February 2022. 'German Court Orders Adler Short-Seller To Cut False Details From Research Report'. Guenther Walcher, who controls Aggregate (a large shareholder of Adler), won a court case against short seller Viceroy that his connections with Caner were not what Viceroy was saying. Also, he only had 0.13% involvement via the bonds of Level One in the past. According to Bloomberg: 'However, the order hasn't yet been enforced because court authorities have had difficulty in officially notifying Viceroy and Perring, who maintain legal addresses outside Europe, so the language is still in the online version of the Viceroy report'.[1] So, you win a court case

and then you cannot enforce it! Bloomberg again: 'In the ruling, the judges took aim at Viceroy's claim that Walcher was "a major investor in Caner's Level One company" and that "Aggregate was allegedly carrying out Caner's instruction to the letter," citing former Aggregate employees. Level One was a company owned by Caner that collapsed more than a decade ago'.

Disclaimer of Opinion

29 April 2022. 'Adler Group S.A. today received notice from the auditor, KPMG Luxembourg Société Anonyme, that as a result of the audit a disclaimer of opinion for the consolidated financial statements and the annual accounts 2021 will be issued. The auditor has not been able to obtain sufficient appropriate audit evidence to provide a basis for an audit opinion on these annual accounts. The company will publish its audited consolidated financial statements and its audited annual accounts 2021 on 30 April 2022 and therewith comply with the reporting obligations under the terms of its outstanding bonds'. A disclaimer issued means the accounts are audited but not 'fully' approved. It did not trigger a bond default, but it did hit confidence in the group (again). It felt to me that KPMG was unwilling or scared to give strong opinions.

Results Published on a Saturday

30 April 2022. Today (Saturday! Never seen that before!) Adler published its FY results: the last day possible to avoid breach of its bonds. KPMG cited the following reason for the disclaimer: 'The denial of access to certain related party information'. The whole board tendered their resignation, but board members Thilo Schmid and Zinnöcker will stay (asked by Kirsten) for the continuity of the business until the Annual General Meeting on 29 June 2022 and then stand for re-election. The second CEO Beaudemoulin will become sole CEO. On 2 May, the first trading day since results: share price

(Continued)

> *(Continued)*
>
> crashed 29.2% to €5.12, market. The second CEO Beaudemoulin will crashed 29.2% to €5.12, market capitalisation €602 million.
>
> ## Another Bizarre Event
>
> 17 May 2022. Another bizarre day! In the morning, Adler announced a new (interim) CFO, some new corporate governance measures, a €1 billion goodwill impairment at development company Consus, no dividend to be paid, and (now it comes) that the board would like to propose to the AGM that KPMG will again be the auditor for the next book year (2022).
>
> In the morning, Kirsten told the press and investors that Adler would 'take all steps' to resolve questions on the 2021 audit as soon as possible and receive an unqualified audit for its 2022 results. He sounded confident that KPMG would be the auditor for 2022.
>
> However, after the investor call, KPMG told the company that 'they are not available as auditors to Adler Group in the future'. Oh dear! This looks like revenge by KPMG on Kirsten. Kirsten had clashed with KPMG before as he believed they just kept digging, whilst he had limited time to save the company. In an honest and to-the-point letter to investors, Kirsten said KPMG's move was 'a great surprise', that it was 'disappointing' and 'irritating'. He said he 'misjudged KPMG's clear indications of a continuation of the co-operation', adding he had assumed KPMG's ongoing work for Adler was 'certain' until the firm told them otherwise. The company said it had started the search for a new auditor 'immediately' but would not be able to find one in time for the AGM at the end of June. Clearly not great for the share price: down 12.5% to €5.09 and a market capitalisation of €598 million.

Note

1. Bloomberg (2022) 'Adler Short-Seller told to cut "untruthful" details from report', 15 February. https://www.bloomberg.com/news/articles/2022-02-15/adler-report-author-ordered-to-cut-some-untruthful-details

Chapter 20

Understand the Stock Market (Rules)

Being active on the stock market with real-time pricing and liquidity requires a different tool set to deal with the frequently changing narrative and resulting share price volatility. Time and again, well-regarded direct real estate investors do not succeed on the stock exchange. Be aware of the following specific stock market rules.

Have a Conviction, Listen to the Models

Mr Market will constantly challenge one's views. However, resist the urge to act on FOMO (Fear Of Missing Out). One of the biggest challenges is when the market soars but your stocks do not. Only act if it is justified – supported by your conviction and models – not because of FOMO, greed or impatience. These violent moves can also retreat just as quickly if they are not justified.

Be Proactive

The goal should be to stay ahead of the competition, including analysts, by being continuously out there: site visits, detailed analysis and interaction with management teams and other market participants, such as banks, developers, private equity players, retailers and real estate brokers. When I started in June 2000 at the Debt Origination department of ABN AMRO, the literally enormous and sympathetic Douglas Grobbe would say: 'If the phone rings more than once, you are fired!' And when I landed at Equity Research later, the favourite slogan was: 'We write tomorrow's newspapers'. The goal was to be proactive, not reactive.

Analysts Not Good at Spotting 'Turning' Points

Research analysts are perfect cheerleaders of a bull or bear market. Recently, it has happened again. In 2022, real estate stocks started to fall sharply as a result of rising rates and the risk of recession. Once they were down 30–40%, many research houses came through with downgrades on the sector. Although there may still be further downside, they clearly missed the bulk of it. It is in these circumstances, when everyone is turning negative, that it is time to wonder whether it is not time to turn a bit more constructive again. The answer is often 'not yet', but we are typically getting closer to that point of maximum pessimism. Obviously, the same happens in bull markets, when stocks or sometimes whole sectors get cheered on to eternity, such as logistics until the start of 2022, when the party suddenly ended. As Jim Gibson, CEO of Big Yellow, says: 'If an investor had done the opposite of what the analysts recommended over the past 20 years, we would have been very rich!'

When Management Teams Are Upset ...

It may sound awkward, but it does happen – management teams who are extremely upset with their share price and capital markets in general. I have seen management teams publicly complaining about how the market is treating them or what certain analysts are saying about them: 'They don't understand our business! They are so wrong! They forget we are …'. The interesting thing: there is often an inverse relationship between how

Understand the Stock Market (Rules)

severely management is upset about how the market is treating them and whether they are right.

At the start of 2022, the management of a German residential property company was very upset with equity markets: 'German house prices won't go down! The market is overreacting!' Many market participants (including me) believed the market had it right and management had been naïve. To be frank, I know very few executives who can truly spot an upcoming downturn or how valuation multiples will move in the future. Don't rely too much on them. It is better to have your own models and view. It comes back to this Stockholm syndrome for real estate, but it is also about missing the wider (macro) picture.

At JP Morgan, I gave presentations to investors all over the world, and it was sometimes striking to see that the (London and New York) financial community had already accepted that the market had fundamentally shifted a while ago, whilst others elsewhere were still in their little bubble or downbeat sentiment. It often takes time for a paradigm shift to occur within the broader investment community.

Every Day Is a New Day

Every day presents a fresh opportunity. Technically, you can sell your entire portfolio daily and begin anew with a clean slate. Each day, I ask myself: 'If I were starting today with a clean sheet, would I still buy these stocks, and in these quantities?' This practice helps me remain objective, ensuring I haven't become overly attached to certain stocks or overlooked others. Sentimentality has no place in investing. Adopting a clean sheet approach also helps in accepting losses more rationally. Don't dwell on past mistakes; they're part of the investment journey. The key is to be right more often than wrong. You can recover from setbacks; what matters is how you handle them.

Have a Wish List

It's crucial to maintain a list of quality companies – those with great assets, a strong balance sheet and excellent management. These might be too expensive today, but you should be ready to buy if their share prices drop significantly. The fundamental research should already be completed, and the wish list prepared.

The World Wants to Move Forward

Some investors are perpetually bearish. While it is important to be critical, living with a constant negative outlook is not for me. I've had negative stances at times during my career, only to see that the world tends to move forward eventually. Remember this: being critical is essential, but maintaining a degree of optimism is equally important. Things will improve, and it's rational to be optimistic.

Can Management (and You!) Present a Convincing Business Case with Numbers in One Minute?

In my experience, if management teams can passionately present the investment case clearly and simply within one minute, it strongly indicates that the company might be an attractive investment. This is especially true if there are multiple levers of value creation and the case is supported by an easy 'back-of-the-envelope' calculation showing significant upside for the shares.

Kitchen Sinking and Conservative Guidance

It is common for a new CEO to paint a more negative picture of the current situation to highlight improvements later on. This can include taking significant write-downs and costs upfront, a practice known as 'kitchen sinking'. When management teams provide guidance, such as profit predictions for the next 12 months, it is often conservative. This allows them to potentially exceed expectations (which is positive news for the market and builds their track record) and ensures that minor setbacks don't immediately lead to downgraded outlooks (which markets dislike and can harm their track record).

Sometimes, companies offer long-term guidance, such as predicting over 5% earnings growth per year for the next 5 years or doubling the portfolio size within 5–10 years. Interestingly, these goals are rarely achieved due to unforeseen events. Therefore, I am not a fan of long-term guidance.

The Market Is Lazy and Does Not Reward Complex Companies and Long-Term Developments

The equity market is lazy. It tends to give premium valuations to easy-to-understand, clean companies. Typically, it does not fully reward small companies (why bother), complexity (e.g. companies with multiple business lines, different reporting or complicated financing instruments) or long-term projects like developments (they are frequently only rewarded when they are almost ready).

Don't Be Too Eager Picking Up Stocks in a Downturn

Do not be too quick to pick up property stocks in a downturn: don't catch a falling knife. The well-respected former sell-side analysts at Morgan Grenfell – Adrian Elwood (who later set up the fund manager Clerkenwell Securities) together with Alec Pelmore and Robert Fowlds, who became a top-ranked team at Kleinwort Benson and then at Merrill Lynch (later Bank of America) – observed in the late 1980s/early 1990s downturn that when a real estate stock slumped 50%, it would typically halve again. The stock market crash of 1987 and the property crash of 1989/1990 resulted in 30 corporate failures, mainly trader developers, out of the 60 listed property stocks under their coverage. So don't be too eager! Typically, there is still leverage risk and overshooting risk in the system.

Watch Out for the Wallstreet Crowd!

During my time at JP Morgan, meeting investors, particularly in New York, it became evident that investment ideas are widely shared among hedge fund investors. This often led to strong waves of buyers or sellers based on the same theme. For instance, buying German residential stocks when the market was fundamentally very cheap, or selling shopping centre stocks expecting them to decline due to e-commerce. I believe these waves were based on solid themes, but their sheer force meant that even if the thesis wasn't entirely accurate, the weight of money would make it work.

Right or not, the stocks would move, potentially intimidating other market participants who would hesitate to bet against it. In my experience, these waves often resulted in significant over- or undershooting of share prices. If you were part of the wave, you had to ensure you were not the last one leaving the party.

The Psychology of Numbers and Patterns

If a share price plummets by 50%, it would have to rise 100% to return to its initial level (assuming that level still holds). You lose 50% if you invest at the top, but you would gain 100% if you bought at the low. The upside increases exponentially as the share price falls, something that becomes very apparent during downturns (Figure 20.1). Simple number crunching, but important to keep in mind.

A steadily rising share price feels better than one that plummets first and then rises to the same level as the steady gainer. The former pattern feels more reassuring than one that rockets upwards sharply and then falls back. There is a thought that if the current dip is not as severe as the previous one, it is okay to stick with it, but if it is worse, it is time to sell. All these share price patterns may end at the same level, but higher volatility is typically associated with higher risk, while large downward movements can make you worry you might be missing something.

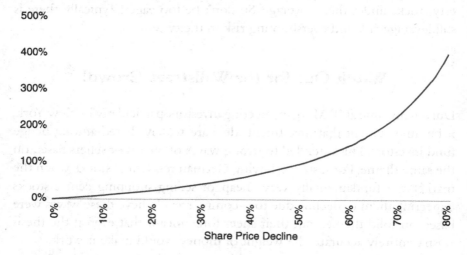

Figure 20.1 Required rebound to break even
Source: Author.

Activism or Company Repositioning Takes Time

It is good to be an active shareholder, but keep in mind that significant lucrative change is often only achieved if an activist (a) can exercise a high degree of control over the situation; (b) has ways to make management and the board move, i.e. management cannot hide behind the law or are sensitive to a public campaign, and (c) can easily exit once goals are achieved.

Exploiting the Reversal Patterns for Similar Companies

Property stocks within the same sector tend to move in reversal patterns. For example, it has been remarkable how closely the share prices of the two retail stocks presented in Figure 20.2 have tracked each other over time. When one strongly outperforms the other, such as Eurocommercial Properties (ECP) outperforming Klépierre, the other tends to catch up eventually. Thus, it would be optimal to sell ECP and buy Klépierre instead (as shown in Figure 20.2 when the '120 level' was broken).

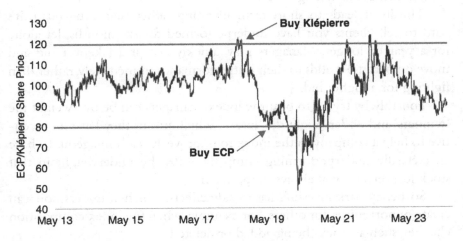

Figure 20.2 Trading pattern – ECP versus Klépierre
Source: Adapted from FactSet.

Benefit from Benchmark Investors

There are numerous funds focused on listed real estate, but almost all of them aim to 'beat' a benchmark index of European listed property companies. These benchmark funds can clearly be beneficial for investors assembling a broad, liquid market portfolio with a reduced risk profile. However, there are also side effects.

Firstly, as previously discussed, while there are around 400 listed real estate companies in Europe, only 103 are in the European Public Real Estate Association (EPRA) Europe Index, 80% of the index made up of just the top 40 companies. This means many fund managers do not need to pay attention to approximately 360 companies. Fund managers don't really care, brokers don't really care and bankers don't really care. As a result, many companies do not receive proper attention and are often overlooked, even though they can be very attractive investments. The lack of attention also means many companies cannot grow further and risk getting stuck.

Secondly, benchmarks create herd behaviour. Not all fund managers dare to stand out. They buy stocks because others are buying them, prices go up or they cannot afford to underperform for too long. Yes, the trend may break at some point, but it's safer to be wrong with everyone else than to risk being wrong alone.

Thirdly, it leads to short-term investing rather than long-term. It's hard to tell clients you have underperformed for six months, let alone for a year or longer. Managers may quickly accept a takeover bid and move on because it adds to their outperformance immediately, rather than fighting for a higher bid.

Fourthly, by trying to beat the index, managers can be overweight the 'winners' and underweight the 'losers', which means they have no incentive to help a company in the index to improve. It is advantageous to have an eternally underperforming company – just be underweight in that stock forever, and you always outperform.

So, benchmark investing has its side effects, which, if understood, can create opportunities for others. For example, when the index composition changes, such as stocks being added or deleted.

Monitor Insider Trading and Shareholder Notifications

When a company insider trades in its shares, they must notify the market, and a statement is issued. It is worthwhile to monitor the share trading activities of these insiders, particularly when conducted by an executive or non-executive with a strong long-term track record. For me, sizeable insider trading has often been a stronger signal than share buybacks, probably because it indicates managers are really putting their money where their mouth is.

However, I often call the managers to find out the reasoning behind a purchase or sale, as there might be a specific reason, e.g. it might be related to an earlier commitment to buy shares or sell them for tax reasons or divorce. Equally, a lack of insider trading for a very long time might indicate that the managers can't trade because a major transaction such as an acquisition or takeover is pending. It can provide an extra piece of the puzzle.

Good luck!
Harm Meijer
December 2024

Acknowledgements

This book would not have come together without the help of many others.

I am deeply indebted and grateful for the cooperation of many high-profile investment professionals, who entrusted their wisdom, rules for success and lessons to me. I conducted many interviews. In particular, I would like to thank Sir Stelios Haji-Ioannou, Yakir Gabay, Guillaume Poitrinal, Evert Jan van Garderen, Jim Gibson, Nicholas Vetch, Soumen Das, Toby Courtauld, Andrew Jones, Andrew Coombs, Sir John Ritblat, Jamie Ritblat, Alec Pelmore, Roberts Fowlds, Alan Carter, Philip Charls, Jaap Tonckens, Remco Simon, Dirk Philippa, Rob Oosterkamp, Rutger van der Lubbe, Michiel te Paske and Rogier Quirijns for their insights.

I have the deepest appreciation for all my colleagues over the years, who had to put up with me and my continuous strive to improve and keep pushing higher and higher. With hindsight, I might have driven them crazy with my passion and morning greeting 'Another day in paradise!' (while everybody was exhausted). Thank you for sticking with me, for which I am forever grateful.

ACKNOWLEDGEMENTS

It all began in 1998, when I started my first job as a trainee at the Amsterdam Exchanges (AEX). The Research Department head Mark Adema gave me just one word: Property. What kind of property-related products could AEX introduce to the market? This word would change my career path and life forever. Thank you Mark!

During my time at ABN AMRO, I bumped into two chaps, Remco Vinck and Ward Kastrop. They were inseparable, but were great teachers for me: don't bullshit, do your work, dress properly (one day I was badly told off for wearing socks from an airplane as I did not have any clean ones left, and to buy a nice suit) and present properly. I learned a lot from them, including to analyse the underlying real estate markets in detail, e.g. by constructing a model to predict future vacancy in offices or retailer sales per square metre in shopping centres.

Andrew Penny and James Muir persuaded me to come to London, which proved to be life-changing. When I started in Equity Research at JP Morgan in 2005, I inherited a Kiwi, who lived most of his youth in Australia: Tim Leckie. We got off to a rough start. We ended up shouting at each other on a full research floor. That was not great, to say the least. We agreed that if one was not happy with the other, he would say: 'Let's go for a coffee (outside)…'. I think this only occurred once or twice. We would become a great team and, more importantly, great friends. Later (over different time periods) Osmaan Malik, Peter Papadakos, Annelies Vermeulen and Neil Green would join the JP Morgan real estate team. We worked hard, went for it, saw it all (boom and bust), but also had fun. I am very proud though, as all of them ended up as great analysts with leading roles in the industry. A special mention here for the head of research at JP Morgan at that time, Jose Linares, who understood the real estate product and was always supportive. Without him, my future would not have been the same.

In 2010, JP Morgan would merge with the posh UK investment bank Cazenove. One of the new sales guys called me over and told me he had this amazing specialist sales for the real estate team. I was suspicious, fearing I got a leftover dumped in my team. It was John van Marle. However, my concerns were totally misplaced. He would become the best specialist sales in the sector and great cheerleader of our research product, for which I am deeply indebted. For years he was a great sounding board and we together met high-profile investors all over the world, although I must have frequently bored John with my endless theories and opinions on real estate!

Acknowledgements

I am grateful to my ICAMAP partners and colleagues. My French partners, Guillaume Poitrinal and Alexandre Aquien, have broadened my real estate and financial markets knowledge. Our continued strive to move forward made me a more complete real estate professional. My direct colleagues have been instrumental in the development of ICAMAP and (therefore also) the book: Alessandro Pagliaro, Luke Green, Carlo Wiegand, Hanna Rollman, Sara Neguillo Selfa and interns Sunny Chada and Koen Philippa. A big thanks for your input and/or feedback, especially to Carlo who helped me in his free time with the charts and tables.

I am forever thankful for the investors in the ICAMAP funds. Without you, I could not have fulfilled my dreams and grown further in this industry.

I am also highly indebted to Michiel te Paske, Richard Mayers, Peter Papadakos and Alison Jones for reading the manuscript. Your critical comments have truly enriched the book.

Peter Woodifield did a terrific job in improving my Dutch English! He was patient and enhanced my script significantly.

Writing a book is one thing, getting it published is another, but thankfully authors Peter Bill, Chris Kane and especially my godfather Fik Meijer and Andrea Carpenter were truly good-hearted with their advice and introductions.

There are many others I have to thank. For example, Chris Ward, formerly COO of Shaftesbury Capital, who kindly sent me Oliver Marriott's book *The Property Boom*; the European Public Real Estate Association (EPRA) organization, under the leadership of Dominique Moerenhout, which is always there to help with data queries; Patrick Long and James Jacobs, who kindly invite me to their industry-leading investment dinners, and Sebastiaan van Loon, who also generously extends similar invitations; Nils Kok and Piet Eichholtz of Maastricht University, who invited me to speak for the Global Real Estate Leaders Program in collaboration with MIT Boston, which was a good test for the book, and Menno Oosterhoff, who came up with the title. If I have missed any stories or omitted someone, please inform me, and I will endeavour to include them in future editions.

I would also like to extend my heartfelt gratitude to the publishing team at Wiley, whose dedication, professionalism, and expertise transformed this manuscript into the book it is today. From editing to design and marketing, their efforts were invaluable in bringing this project to fruition. In particular, I would like to acknowledge Gemma Valler

(Commissioning Editor), Alice Hadaway (Editorial Assistant), Susan Cerra (Senior Managing Editor), Elaine Bingham (Copy Editor), Kalaivanthan Jayaraman (Content Refinement Specialist), and Katy Smith (Publicity Manager) for their exceptional contributions.

I would also like to draw attention to great industry people who unfortunately were taken away from the colourful world of real estate too early: François Bacchetta, Ian Coull, Graham Roberts, Ron Spinney, Rodney Zimmerman, Henk Postma, Oginda Vlijter, Anders Nissen, Marjan Hogeslag, Thom Wernink and most recently industry figurehead Léon Bressler.

Writing this book has been a long process and could not have been done without true friends and family. I extend my gratitude to my friends (and a special mention for Peer, who believes he added great value), Dave, my sisters and brothers. Thank you to my parents, who never stop caring about me. I have the best mum I could have wished for. Unfortunately, my father left me too early, but I know you are still looking after me. Finally, a big thanks to my amazing supportive wife Irma and children. Thank you for your support and making my life complete.

Appendix I: Some Terminology

Benchmark: An index of listed companies. The weighting of the stocks in the index is based on the tradeable size of the companies (also called the free float of the market capitalisation). The industry – and its consultants – has an obsession with outperforming the index. The FTSE EPRA Nareit Developed Europe Index (or EPRA Europe) is one of the most well-known indices and included the following companies as of May 2024: abrdn European Logistics Income, abrdn Investment Management, Aedifica, AEW UK REIT, Allreal Holding, ARGAN, Aroundtown, Ascencio, Assura, Atrium Ljungberg, Big Yellow, British Land, CA Immobilien, Care Property, Carmila, Castellum, Catena, Cibus Nordic, Citycon, CLS Holdings, Cofinimmo, Corem Property, Covivio, Custodian REIT, Derwent London, Deutsche EuroShop, Deutsche Wohnen, Dios Fastigheter, Empiric Student Property, Entra, Eurocommercial Properties, Fabege, Fastighets Balder, FastPartner, Gecina, Grainger, Grand City Properties, Great Portland Estates, Hamborner REIT, Hammerson, Helical, Home Invest Belgium, Hufvudstaden, ICADE, Immobiliare Grande Distribuzione, Impact Healthcare, Inmobiliaria Colonial, Intershop Holding,

207

Irish Residential Properties, Klepierre, Kojamo, Land Securities, Lar Espana, LEG Immobilien, Life Science REIT, Logistea B, London-Metric, Mercialys, Merlin Properties, Mobimo, Montea, NewRiver REIT, NP3 Fastigheter, NSI, Nyfosa, Pandox, Peach Property, PHP, Picton Property, Platzer Fastigheter, PRS REIT, PSP Swiss Property, Regional REIT, Residential Secure Income, Retail Estates, Safestore, SAGAX, SBB, Schroder REIT, SEGRO, Shaftesbury, Shurgard, Sirius Real Estate, Supermarket Income, Swiss Prime Site, TAG Immobilien, Target Healthcare, Triple Point Social Housing, Tritax Big Box, Tritax Eurobox, Unibail-Rodamco-Westfield, Unite, Urban Logistics, Vastned Retail, VGP, Vonovia, Wallenstam, Warehouse, WDP, Wereldhave, Wihlborgs Fastigheter, Workspace, Xior Student Housing.

EPRA: European Public Real Estate Association, which represents European-listed property companies, strives to improve its standards and stimulate the creation of REITs. Listed companies are publicly traded on a stock exchange. Other terms for 'listed' are 'public' or 'indirect'. The listed sector is a colourful, under-researched and under-appreciated segment on the stock exchange.

Financial leverage: Debt used to finance the purchase of real estate. To measure how much debt has been taken on, different financial ratios can be used, e.g. loan-to-value (LTV: net debt divided by the value of the property) and net debt to EBITDA. Some industry participants are addicted to debt.

GFC: Great Financial Crisis (see Appendix III).

Initial Public Offering (IPO): The process of listing a new company on the stock exchange.

Leverage multiplier: The more debt a company has, the more it will gain/lose from property valuation increases or declines. The ratio is calculated as portfolio value divided by its equity. For example, assume a simple finance structure of a property portfolio with a value of 100, financed by 60 debt and 40 equity. Its LTV is 60% (60/100) and the leverage multiplier is 2.5 (100/40). If the building rises/declines by 10%, the multiplier tells you that the equity (= your money) jumps/falls by 25% (10% times 2.5).

Like-for-like: Annual growth in rental income or property values is frequently expressed as like-for-like rental growth/capital growth, which means that exactly the same portfolio is compared to the previous year, i.e. sales/purchases or developments are excluded, and the same square metre space.

Appendix I: Some Terminology

Net asset value (NAV): The equity of the company in its accounts, simply calculated as the value of the portfolio (appraised by an external valuer) minus the net debt of the company (debt minus cash). There are different ways to calculate the NAV, with the EPRA NTA (net tangible assets) being the most widely used. This measure also corrects for any goodwill, purchasers' costs and deferred taxes – if it is likely that those will have to be paid given the company's strategy. The industry is so obsessed with NAV that it is hampering its growth.

Recurring earnings/profit: This is the profit generated from the rental income from the real estate. It is calculated as gross rental income received minus operating costs, overhead costs, interest expenses and taxes – if any. The gross rent minus operating costs is called the net rental income. The net rental income minus the overhead costs is named EBITDA (earnings before interest payments, depreciation and amortisation).

REIT: Real estate investment trust. There are various REIT regimes in the world, each with their own rules, but the bottom line is that a REIT does not pay any taxes on income or capital gains in return for paying out a required minimum dividend every year, typically at least 75% of recurring earnings, on which typically dividend tax is due. REITs have institutionalised the opaque real estate sector by bringing transparency and liquidity.

Reversionary potential/under-rented: The percentage the market rent is higher than the current rent paid. If the market rent is lower than the current rent, we call the property over-rented.

Total return: The total return from an asset comprises the rental income and change in value of the property, adjusted for costs. The total return of property shares on the stock exchange is a function of change in share price plus any dividend payments received.

Yield: Expressed as rental income (gross or net) divided by the market value of the property, including or excluding costs for purchasing the asset, e.g. agent costs and any transfer duties. It is a yardstick frequently used in real estate, e.g. party X bought the office on a yield of 5%. A high yield is typically a reflection of a weaker or more secondary asset, whilst high potential or prime real estate is valued at lower yields. If Yield = Rent divided by Value, it follows that Value = Rent divided by Yield. This is one way to value a property. Another way would be to use a Discounted Cash Flow Model (DCFM) that incorporates forecast cash flows for the next 5/10 years, which are discounted back to today.

Yield compression/yield expansion: If demand for real estate is high, the valuation yield on real estate valuations falls. This is called 'yield compression'. Everything else being equal, the value of the properties rises. The opposite is called 'yield expansion', which happened when interest rates started to rise in 2022. Everything else being equal, prices fall.

Yield sensitivity: Lower-yielding properties are more sensitive to changes in yield assumptions than higher-yielding assets. When a valuation yield compresses from 4% to 3%, the value rises by 33.3% (4%/3% − 1)! If the leverage multiplier is 2, the equity rockets upwards by a whopping 66.7% (33.3% times 2)! If, however, the yield on a property is 8% and compresses to 7%, the price would 'only' rise by 14.3% (8%/7% − 1) and the equity by 28.6%. These examples clearly show the power of yield compression combined with leverage. This process of falling yields combined with leverage occurred in real estate after the Great Financial Crisis of 2007/2009 (GFC; see Appendix III for a detailed description of this period) and during the COVID period up till 2022, as central banks hugely stimulated financial markets/economies. Obviously, the situation can also escalate in a negative way with yields expanding. For example, if the yield grows from 3% to 4%, the value drops by 25% and the equity by 50%, assuming the same leverage multiplier of 2. The latter happened with German residential property in 2022/2023, when central banks started to withdraw money supply from the system, e.g. by raising interest rates.

Appendix II:
Six Basic Valuation Metrics Explained

Discount to NAV	Definition	Measures the discount or premium the listed equity market assigns to the book equity. The book equity is based on the appraisal value of the portfolio.
	Calculation	**Formula: Share Price/NAV per Share−1** NAV per Share is calculated by taking the external appraisal valuation of the real estate portfolio, subtracting net debt to get the company's NAV, and dividing this NAV by the number of outstanding shares.
	Adjustments	NAV can be adjusted for factors such as the market value of debt or deferred taxes, especially if real estate is expected to be sold in due course.

211

APPENDIX II: SIX VALUATION METRICS

Dividend Yield

Definition — Measures the annual declared dividend (payment to investors) as a percentage of the share price.

Calculation — **Formula: Dividend per Share/Share Price**

Earnings Yield

Definition — Measures the recurring earnings as a percentage of the share price.

Calculation — **Formula: Recurring Earnings Per Share (EPS)/Share Price**

Recurring earnings from the company's profit and loss (P&L) account focus on the rental business, calculated as gross rental income minus operating costs, overhead costs, interest expenses and any taxes related to the rental business.

Notes

1. Excludes items such as revaluation, non-recurring development or sales profits/losses, or results on derivatives.
2. P&L may include non-cash elements, e.g. rent-free periods not yet received in cash. Recurring earnings can be calculated using cash items only (called Funds From Operations, FFO) or adjusted for additional recurring capital expenditure not captured in the P&L (Adjusted Funds From Operations, AFFO).

Implied EBITDA Yield

Definition — Measures the implied portfolio yield, i.e. the net yield after overhead costs at which the equity market values the portfolio.

Calculation — **Formula: EBITDA/Enterprise Value (EV)**

EV is calculated as:
- Net debt plus equity market capitalisation.
- Equity market capitalisation is computed by multiplying the outstanding number of shares by the share price.

Notes — Various yields can be calculated, e.g. using gross or net rental income (after operating costs but before overhead costs) instead of EBITDA.

Appendix II: Six Valuation Metrics

Discount to GAV	**Definition**	Measures the discount or premium the listed equity market assigns to the portfolio valuation. This differs from the discount to NAV, as it is an 'ungeared' discount.
	Calculation	**Formula: EV/GAV (Gross Asset Value)−1** GAV is the appraisal value of the portfolio.
	Notes	Adjustments should be made for other business lines, such as development, to arrive at a discount for the operating portfolio.
Implied Price per Sqm	**Definition**	Measures the price per square metre at which the equity market values the portfolio.
	Calculation	**Formula: EV/Total Square Metres**
	Notes	Adjustments should be made for other activities, such as development.

Appendix III:
The Great Financial
Crisis (GFC)

I mention the Great Financial Crisis (GFC) frequently in this book because the real estate markets collapsed spectacularly, profoundly impacting the industry. There was an enormous overhang of properties, often held by banks, as the property values were frequently less than the outstanding debt. Cleaning up this mess required significant time and effort, resulting in slow and wobbly economic growth – a painful period.

The GFC was preceded by a property price boom that began after the dot-com bubble burst at the start of the millennium, driven by loose monetary conditions combined with economic growth. However, the party ended when the US subprime mortgage crisis hit. Falling house prices started to expose dubious financing structures, such as mortgage-backed securities (MBS) and collateralised debt obligations (CDOs), which affected financial institutions worldwide. These financially engineered products were filled with so-called NINJA (No Income, No Job, No Assets) loans, a slang term for high-risk borrowers unlikely to

215

repay the interest or principal in the long term. Some institutions failed, with Lehman Brothers being the most famous, but all of them frantically reduced lending to real estate. A severe recession followed. Real estate markets are cyclical by nature and can suffer from overbuilding, as seen in certain sectors in the early 1990s, but that was not *the* driver during the GFC.

The GFC itself roughly covers the period from mid-2007 to Q1 2009, during which real estate markets saw severe declines in values. For example, UK house prices and European commercial real estate values fell by circa 20%, UK commercial property by 30%, and Spanish house prices slumped by 40%; in certain cities, they were even down by 50%, and land prices fell by 75% or more. For most properties, there was simply not even a bid – they were unsellable. As such, the 'real' low was often much lower than published.

The boom and bust were also mirrored in the performance of listed real estate stocks, which staged a huge rally of 284% from the low on 12 March 2003 to the peak on 19 February 2007, after which they fell by 77% to their low on 9 March 2009 – 8% below the start of the rally after the dot-com bubble (Figure A.1).

An impression of the main events and mood in the sector before, during and after the GFC, with key quotes from company annual reports, follows.

Figure A.1 European Public Real Estate Association (EPRA) Europe – total return
Source: Author, FactSet.

2004 – Cheap Credit

Following the dot-com crash, the Federal Reserve lowered the federal funds rate from 6.5% in May 2000 to 1% in June 2003, providing an opportunity to take on cheap debt. This marked the beginning of renewed interest in real estate.

> Given a reasonable economic climate, property will benefit because capitalisation rates are having the long overdue correction I forecast. . . . The merits of property for investors have once more been widely appreciated since the stock market shakeout following the dotcom frenzy.
>
> —*Sir John Ritblat, Chairman, British Land,*
> *annual report 2004*

> Yields tightening in all our markets, reflecting strong investment demand for commercial property assets.
>
> —*Peter Birch, Chairman, Land Securities*
> *(now Landsec), annual report 2004*

2005 – Securitisation

Innovative financing structures have been on the rise, including securitisation, where various sorts of mortgages are packaged together and grouped in different classes with their own risk and return profile, such as residential or commercial mortgage-backed securities. Property prices are rising fast; for example, British Land reported 32% net asset value (NAV) growth driven by a 14% increase in property valuations and development gains during its financial year ending March 2006. The sector is excited, although there is some caution about the high rate of growth.

> There is further evidence of yield compression in the early part of 2006 but the indications are that this is not likely to be as sustained as we experienced in 2005.
>
> —*Ian Coull, CEO, Slough Estates (now SEGRO),*
> *annual report 2005*

Whilst the recent rate of growth in capital values is unlikely to be sustained, demand for prime property investments remains strong.

—*John Nelson, Chairman, Hammerson,*
annual report 2005

2006 – Strong Valuation Growth

Real estate companies continue to report strong growth in property valuations of around 10%, with Hammerson up almost 15%. Nevertheless, the tone becomes less bullish in the sector, but few really saw what was coming.

We also do not believe that the unprecedented levels of growth in property values will continue at the same rate or necessarily be sustainable across all property types, particularly more secondary buildings.

—*Peter Birch, Chairman, Land Securities,*
annual report 2006

Expect growth rates to reduce, whilst remaining both positive and competitive with other asset classes on a risk-adjusted basis.

—*Stephen Hester, CEO, British Land,*
annual report 2006

During 2006 demand from investors for real estate in the UK and France was buoyant, particularly during the first half of the year, leading to further appreciation in capital values. We expect continued demand from a broad range of investors for prime investment properties. However, following the recent increases in interest rates in both countries, the positive differential between property investment yields and borrowing costs has been largely eliminated or reversed, reducing the attractiveness of property to some debt-financed investors. Against this background, we believe that capital growth in 2007 will depend more on asset management initiatives and increases in rental income than a further downward movement in investment yields.

—*John Nelson, Chairman, Hammerson, annual report 2006*

2007 – Credit Crisis

Values started to decline as the subprime crisis emerged, credit conditions tightened and confidence eroded. On 1 October 2007, UBS became the first major bank to announce losses ($3.4 billion) from subprime-related investments. Central banks took coordinated action by providing billions of dollars in loans to global credit markets (key date: August 2007, the fall of Northern Rock in the UK). The real estate sector began to reel.

> Events in the markets around us, following the US subprime crisis and subsequent credit crunch, cannot be ignored.
>
> *—Guillaume Poitrinal, CEO, Unibail-Rodamco (now URW),*
> *annual report 2007*

> After several years of buoyant property markets and yield compression in all classes of property, 2007 saw the erosion of confidence in the sector as the credit crunch affected financial markets.
>
> *—Nigel Rich, Chairman, Slough Estates (now SEGRO),*
> *annual report 2007*

> On the one hand, for the time being our core West End market appears to be holding up, on the other, there is no question that a deep-seated sense of fragility and uncertainty pervades and this is not going to disappear overnight.
>
> *—Richard Peskin, Chairman, Great Portland Estates (now GPE),*
> *annual report 2008*

2008 – Lehman Collapse

In March 2008, Bear Stearns was acquired by JP Morgan Chase for cents on the dollar. In September, Fannie Mae and Freddie Mac were seized by the US Government, and Lehman Brothers collapsed (with $639 billion in assets and $619 billion in debt). The public questioned the financial health of banks and withdrew their money, amplifying liquidity problems.

220 APPENDIX III: THE GREAT FINANCIAL CRISIS (GFC)

The collapse of Lehman Brothers in the Autumn of 2008, closely followed by the need for emergency action by governments to provide equity capital and other support to several banks, increased the uncertainties. The consequence was a very significant downturn in investment activity in property markets in the last quarter of 2008 and further falls in values, with the effect more pronounced in the UK than in France [its property values fell 26% in the UK and 11% in France].

—John Nelson, Chairman, Hammerson, annual report 2008

While the financial crisis has a firm grip on the economic environment, no player in our industry will remain unaffected by the scarcity of available financing or the general economic downturn.

—Olivier Elamine, CEO, alstria office REIT-AG,
annual report 2008

2009 – Balance Sheet Revival (Rights Issues)

Real estate companies remained under pressure due to tight credit markets. To repair their balance sheets and avoid debt covenant breaches, many UK companies turned to rights issues to raise capital from the equity markets. Available capital remained scarce, but values seemed to have hit the bottom in many markets, although the recovery would be slow and uneven between sectors and countries.

This put us in a position to join the other major listed property companies in going to our shareholders with a rights issue at the beginning of March. With the support of our shareholders, we raised £500 million and put our balance sheet back on a secure footing.

—Nigel Rich, Chairman, SEGRO, annual report 2009

We were the first property company to launch a Rights Issue in response to the rapid decline in property values. We renegotiated the covenants on our debt facilities and extended the terms of our debt to remove any near-term refinancing risk.,.

—Tony Hales, Non-Executive Chairman, Workspace,
annual report 2009

Appendix III: The Great Financial Crisis (GFC)

Our priorities have been clear: to maintain the income stream and reduce costs while tackling the balance sheet.

—Harry Platt, CEO, Workspace, annual report 2009

...the investment market is highly dependent on the availability of financing, and the willingness of banks to provide funding. As long as the banks show limited willingness to finance real estate, it is likely that market conditions will remain challenging.

—Olivier Elamine, CEO, alstria office REIT-AG,
annual report 2009

...the value correction phase seems to be over...

—Michel Clair, Chairman, Klépierre, annual report 2009

2010 – Economic Uncertainty

The beginning of a recovery, with economic uncertainty prevalent throughout Europe, but there were differences in speed between countries: the UK was bleak, as were countries that received bail-out packages, such as Greece, Spain, Portugal and Ireland. Germany was doing better.

It may take the UK economy a number of years to regain full strength.

—Alison Carnwath, Chairwoman, Land Securities,
annual report 2010

...companies with short-term refinancing requirements may continue to find it difficult to secure adequate funding at costs comparable with their existing facilities.

—Hammerson annual report 2010

222 APPENDIX III: THE GREAT FINANCIAL CRISIS (GFC)

…as we are currently seeing, factors such as the lack of available credit and low levels of consumer confidence can depress demand … Lack of liquidity in the banking markets will necessitate changes in our balance sheet structure with reduced dependency on pooled bank debt sources of finance and increased emphasis on recycling capital rather than asset accumulation.

—*Andrew Cunningham, CEO, Grainger, annual report 2010*

Economic conditions are expected to be positive in 2011, which will continue to push tenant demand in the leasing market.

—*Olivier Elamine, CEO, alstria office REIT-AG, annual report 2010*

2011 – Wait and See Attitude

A continuation in asset value recovery, but growth remained slow as investors waited to see how issues would be resolved. Spain was one of the hardest hit real estate markets and continued to struggle.

While, as a nation, we have moved from 'Recession' to the 'Age of Austerity', consumers are still shopping, and good businesses are looking to grow.

—*Chris Gibson-Smith, Chairman, British Land, annual report 2011*

For the period 2013–2015, much will depend on how the economic crisis is going to be resolved.

—*Unibail-Rodamco annual report, annual report 2011*

As is well known, during 2011 the market was very tough. In general, real estate transactions reduced radically, prices were fragile, and the vacancy rate remained unchanged. The financial markets were closed or in a significant downward trend.

—*Pere Viñolas Serra, CEO, Inmobiliaria Colonial, annual report 2010*

2012 – Slow Recovery

Economic uncertainty remained prevalent, resulting in a slow recovery, three years after the trough of the financial crisis. For Spain, which suffered from a large debt hangover, the recovery would start in 2014, later than other countries.

> Economic conditions remain uncertain, although there are some signs of stabilisation in the Eurozone and of a recovery in the UK. Property finance continues to be restricted for many and this, combined with the risk-averse attitude of investors, means that the pricing of secondary assets is likely to remain under pressure.
>
> —*David Sleath, CEO, SEGRO, annual report 2012*

> The year 2012 was marked by a deterioration in the macroeconomic climate in Europe, particularly in Spain, with an evolution that some economists classify as the 'W', and that postpones the prospects of recovery compared to the expectations that most analysts had two years ago. In this environment, the office markets in Spain have had continual setbacks in their fundamentals, while in France they remained stable.
>
> —*Pere Viñolas Serra, CEO, Inmobiliaria Colonial, annual report 2012*

About the Author

Harm has been active in the real estate sector in various roles for more than 25 turbulent years. He is a well-known figure in the listed European real estate world. After completing his degree in Econometrics, he began his career as a management trainee at the Amsterdam Exchange (AEX) in 1998. There, he witnessed the boom of the dot-com era, financial excesses and the steady professionalisation of the financial and property industries. In 2000, he joined ABN AMRO, where he became a leading research analyst. He then moved to JP Morgan in London, where he became managing director in 2010. There, he experienced the real estate boom, bust and aftermath of the Great Financial Crisis (GFC). During this time, he and his team were ranked number one in European real estate equities research six times between 2008 and 2014 in the well-regarded Institutional Investor survey and five times in a row from 2009 till 2013 in the Extel survey.

In 2013, he co-founded the real estate investment boutique ICAMAP with Guillaume Poitrinal, the successful CEO of Unibail-Rodamco, and Alexandre Aquien. Harm has built up a strong track record in investing in listed European real estate. Additionally, he has served as a non-executive board member of the Dutch office company NSI NV

226

ABOUT THE AUTHOR

and as a non-executive board member and chairman of the hotel company easyHotel. Moreover, he has taught at universities, served on the Reporting and Accountancy Committee of the industry body European Public Real Estate Association (EPRA) for many years and is a frequent panellist and speaker at conferences.

Index

A

acquisition bonus, 113
Adler Group S.A. ('Adler'), 57, 147, 181–92
   Gerresheim development project, 185
   logo, 184
   Wilhelm project, 183
Adler Real Estate, 184
Ado Properties, 184
Aermont, 95
AFFO (Adjusted Funds From Operations), 113
Aggregate, 185, 190, 191
Allianz, 143
alstria office REIT-AG, 220, 221
Amsterdam Exchanges (AEX), 108–9
Amundi Immobilier, 89
annual rent indexation, 30
APG Asset Management, 125
Arnold, John, 101
Aroundtown (AT1), 45
AXA Investment Managers, 86

B

Bank of America, 110, 197
Bank of England (BoE), 20, 56
Beaudemoulin, 191, 192
benchmark, definition, 207
benchmark index, 42, 89, 91, 92, 102,
    156, 157, 200

benchmark investors, 200
Berlin, retail space in, 24–5
Bernanke, Ben, 56
Beta, 50
Big Yellow, 139, 141, 194
Birch, Peter, 217, 218
Blackstone, 10, 52, 144
boards, role of, 100
Bouygues, 88
Branicks Group, 147
Bressler, Léon, 95, 96, 97
British Land, 20, 65, 83, 217, 218, 221
Brixton, 75, 76–8
Brookfield, 10, 52, 144
Brookfield Property Group, 175
bubble check list, 41–3
bubble symptoms, 41–3
Buffett, Warren, 120
Burks, Philip, 141
business as usual mindset, 164

C

Caner, 184, 190, 191
Cap Gemini-Ernst, 86
Capco, 81
Capital & Counties (Capco), 164, 171
Capital & Regional (C&R), 104–5
Capital Asset Pricing Model (CAPM), 50

227

INDEX

Capital Shopping Centres (CSC), 167, 168, 169
  see also intu Properties
Carnwath, Alison, 221
Carter, Alan, 107, 120
cash flow
  focus on, 122–3
  sufficient, 72
CCF-HSBC, 86
central banks, 55–60
  arbitrage opportunities, 559–60
  bail out, 59
  power of, 58
  stimulus or restrictive policy, 59
  volatility, 58–9
CEO, role of, 110–11
Charls, Philip, 103
Chinatown, London, 24
Circle Property Trust, 101–2
Citycon, 74
Clair, Michel, 221
Clerkenwell Securities, 197
closed-ended listed funds (REITs), 6, 63
closed-ended non-listed funds, 6
club-deal, 6
Coeur Défense, 85–90
  distressed sale, 89–90
  financing, 86–7
  letting process, 86
  partial sale, 87
  as Unibail key office development, 85–6
  value creation, 88–9
Cohen & Steers, 61
collateralised debt obligations (CDOs), 215
Columbia Threadneedle Investments, 167
Commercial Mortgage-Backed
      Security (CMBS), 86
company positioning, 137
company voluntary agreements, 164
compounding, rent, 21–2
conservative underwriting, 51–2
Consumer Price Index (CPI), 30
Consus, 192
contrarian investment, 44–5
convertible bonds, 73
Coombs, Andrew, 38, 83
Corio, 24–5
corporate governance, 107–15
  compounding goodwill, 115
  governance dynamics, 110–11
  remuneration, 111–14
  risk management, 109
  transparency, 110
cost ratio, 120

costs
  COVID response, 56
  management, 7
  non-listed funds, 7
  replacement, 44
  vacancy, 19
Coull, Ian, 217
Courtauld, Toby, 35, 45, 90
Covent Garden, London, 24
COVID response cost, 56
CPPIB, 176
Credit Agricole Assurances, 89
Credit Agricole banking group, 89
credit crisis (2007), 219
Crédit Lyonnais, 86
critical analysis, 47
Cross Roads Property Investors, 88
Crossrail, London, 26

D

Das, Soumen, 81
debt buyback, 100
Delancey, 52
demand, 25–6
  competitiveness of area, 25
  macro-economic outlook, 25
  structural trends, 25
  tenant requirements, 25
denominator effect, 11
Deutsche Wohnen, 91, 92
DIC Asset, 147
direct market studies/models, 26–9
  office model, 26–7
  dominance analysis, 27–9
discount to GAV, 128, 129, 130, 213
discount to NAV, 128, 129, 130,
      133–4, 211
Discounted Cash Flow Model (DCFM), 41,
      43, 48–9, 131
Dividend Discount Model (DDM), 131
dividend per share, 108
dividend yield, 128, 129, 130, 212
dividends
  sustainable policy, 162–3
    coverage by operating cash flow, 163
    modest leverage, 163
    resilient dividend policy, 163
  unsustainable, 161–2
dominance analysis, 27–9
dotcom bubble, 39, 134, 215
downturns
  pattern of, 40–1
  picking up stocks in, 197

Index

rights issues value in, 74–6
shortage of capital in, 74

E

earnings per share (EPS), 108, 112
earnings yield, 128, 129, 130, 212
easyHotel, 122
easyJet, 122
EBITDA ratio, 66
EDF Group, 86
Elamine, Olivier, 220, 221
Elizabeth line, London, 26
Elwood, Adrian, 197
environmental, social and governance (ESG)
   initiatives, 7
EPRA, 103, 107, 226
  definition, 208
EPRA Cost Ratio, 121–2
EPRA Europe index, 10, 42, 43, 156,
   179, 200, 216
EPRA net initial yield, 19, 49, 120
EPRA Sweden, 179
EPRA Vacancy, 121, 122
equivalent yield, 19
estimated rental value (ERV), 122
Eurocommercial Properties, 28, 29, 199
European Central Bank (ECB), 9, 56, 96
European listed equity market, 9–10
EVA (economic value added), 81, 82, 132
Evergrande, 36
expected medium-term rental growth, 49
expected return, 48–9

F

Fannie Mae, 219
Fidelity International, 64
financial leverage, 63–9
  definition, 208
  difficulty in reduction of debt ratios, 67–8
  high, 64
  loose or no covenants, 65
  valuation gains, 66–7
  value decline, absorption of, 65–6
financing, 7, 71–6
  alternative, 73
  diversity, 72
  favourable conditions for raising equity, 72–3
  relationships with debt providers, 73
  rights issues value destructive in
    downturns, 74–6
    shortage of capital in downturns, 74
    UK Rights Issues at the end of GFC, 75–6

spread in maturities and lenders, 72
sufficient cash flow, 72
FOMO (Fear Of Missing Out), 193
Forbes, 95
Fowlds, Robert, 110, 197
Frankfurt Stock Exchange, 45
Freddie Mac, 219

G

Gabay, Yakir, 44–5, 63, 82, 114
GAGFAH, 91
Gallardo, Susana, 96
German residential property market, 57
Gibson, Jim, 141, 194
Gibson-Smith, Chris, 222
Global Financial Crisis see Great Financial crisis
golden rules of real estate, 13
Goldman Sachs, 89
  Whitehall Fund, 87
goodwill, 115
Gordon, Sir Donald, 164
Gothaer, 88
GPE, 35, 75
Grand City Properties, 45
Great Financial Crisis (GFC), 20, 27, 39, 51, 64,
   71, 74, 87, 89, 101, 141, 147, 152, 170,
   208, 215–23
  start date of, 41
  UK rights issues at end of, 75
  2004 cheap credits, 217
  2005 securitisation, 217–18
  2006 strong valuation growth, 218
  2007 credit crisis, 219
  2008 Lehman collapse, 219–20
  2009 balance sheet revival (rights
    issues), 220–1
  2010 economic uncertainty, 221–2
  2011 wait and see attitude, 222
  2012 slow recovery, 223
Great Portland Estates (GPE), 219
Green, Luke, 183
Green REIT, 100
Green Street, 93, 173–4
gross value, 19
gross yield, 18

H

Haji-Ioannou, Sir Stelios, 122
Hales, Tony, 220
Hammerson, 75, 152, 174, 175, 218, 220, 221
Helical Bar, 36, 75
herd behavior, 200

230   INDEX

Hester, Stephen, 218
Hilton, 124
historical performance analysis, 127–8
Home REIT, 158
Hubris Index, 103
hybrid bonds (perpetual instruments), 73
hybrid instruments, 73
hyperinflation, risk of, 56

I

I Gigli, Florence, 29
ICAMAP, 110
Iliad, 95
illiquidity of investment, 5
implied EBITDA yield, 128, 129, 130, 212
implied price per sqm, 128, 129, 213
ING, 86
Initial Public Offerings (IPOs), 42, 180
   definition, 208
Inmobilaria Colonial, 221, 222
insider trading, 201
interest cover, 65, 66, 67
internal rate of return (IRR), 31, 53
intu Properties, 163–76
   fundamental challenged, 164–6
   in denial, 166–7
investors, range of, 2, 3
IVG Immobilien, 123–5

J

joint ventures (JVs), 6, 73
Jones, Andrew, 52, 90, 166
JP Morgan, 152, 167, 188, 195, 197
JP Morgan Chase, 219

K

Kirsten, Professor Stefan, 188, 191, 192
kitchen sinking, 196
Kleinwort Benson, 197
Klépierre, 64, 174, 175, 199, 221
KPMG, 23, 124, 176
   investigation into Adler, 185, 187, 192
KPMG Luxembourg Société Anonyme, 191

L

Land Securities (Landsec), 20, 217, 218, 221
Lazari, Christos, 45
Lazari Investments, 45
lease length, 30–1

leasing strategy, 30
Leckie, Tim, 124
Lehman Brothers, 45, 89, 141, 216, 219–20
Lehman Brothers Real Estate Partners, 88
leverage multiplier, definition, 51, 208
Liberty International, 163–76
   see also intu Properties
like-for-like, 49, 114, 174
   definition, 208
liquidity, 7, 9
listed pricing, accuracy of, 9
listed real estate, 134
   advantages of, 8–9
   liquidity of, 9
loan-to-value (LTV) ratio, 51, 65–6, 67–8, 72,
     86, 87, 89, 93–4, 96, 104, 171–2,
     174, 181
location, role of, 23, 24
London City office model, 27
London-Metric, 52
London Stock Exchange (LSE), 164
Lone Star Real Estate Fund III, 89
Lucky Buyer effect, 57

M

M&A (mergers and acquisitions), 90–7
   drawbacks of, 90–1
   potential benefits of, 90
Malik, Osmaan, 123
management and board alignment, 156–9
   compensation packages, 157
   external vs internal management, 157–8
   mindset of, 158–9
   protection measures, 158
management intensity, 7
margin for error, 134–5
Merrill Lynch, 110, 197
Metliss, Cyril, 83–4
Mezzanine, 73
Microsoft, 86
minimum capital expenditure (capex)
   green, 33–4
   tenant incentives, 34
   types of, 33
modelling, 131–2
Moody's, 74, 94
Morgan Grenfell, 197
Morgan Stanley, 86
mortgage-backed securities (MBS), 215
mosaic theory, 125
Mouchel, Fabrice, 97

Index

231

N

NASDAQ, 42, 43
Nelson, John, 218, 220
Neobo Fastigheter, 180
net asset value (NAV), 82, 108, 113, 131–2
  criticisms of, 128
  definition, 209
net debt to EBITDA ratio, 66, 67,
    93, 94, 171–2
net debt to recurring EBITDA ratio, 92
net rent, 18
net yield, 19
Niel, Xavier, 95
NINJA (No Income, No Job, No Assets)
    loans, 215
Northern Rock, 219
NSI, 101

O

office model, 26–7
Olins, Edward, 101
Olyan Group, 175
opacity of investment, 5
open-ended non-listed funds, 6
open outcry, 108, 109
operating cash flow, 72
optimism, 151–3
overconfidence, 103–6

P

pandemic emergency purchase programme
    (PEPP), 56
Parque Principado, Asturias, 170
Peel Group, 168, 169, 175
PEG (price earnings to growth ratio), 131
Pelmore, Alec, 110, 197
PeopleSoft, 86
performance measures, 120–2
  gaming, 112–13
perpetual bonds, 73
Perring, 190
Peskin, Richard, 219
pessimism, 151–3
Phayre-Mudge, Marcus, 167
Philippa, Dirk, 64, 142
Platt, Harry, 221
Poitrinal, Guillaume, 52, 95, 219
portfolio diversification, 6–7
preferred shares, 73
pre-tax profit, 108

price per square foot (price psf), 48
price per square metre (price psm), 48
Primonial REIM, 89
property investment vehicles
  cash flow, focus on, 122–3
  misleading impressions, 119–20
  mosaic theory, 125
property values, cyclical, 39–45
  contrarian side, 44–5
  warning signs, 40–3
    bubble symptoms, 41–3
    Discounted Cash Flow Model (DCFM), 41
    pattern of downturns, 40–1
Puerto Venecia, Zaragoza, 170

Q

Quirijns, Rogier, 61

R

Real Estate Investment Trust *see* REIT
recurring earnings/profit, definition, 209
red flags, 177–8
Regional REIT, 162
REIT, 2, 7, 8, 107, 141
  closed-ended listed funds, 6, 63
  definition, 209
  UK, 75, 76
  US, 157
reload factor, 142
remuneration, 111–14
  gaming, 112–13
  shareholder alignment, 113–14
    annual bonus based on score card, 114
    common sense, 114
    long-term incentive plan focused
      on TSR, 114
    'skin in the game', 114
  spiralling salaries, 111
rent compounding, 21–2
rental contract, type of, 30–2
  contractual uplifts, 30
  lease length, 30–1
  operational performance insight, 30
  tenant churn, 30
rental growth potential, 29–32
  leasing strategy, 30
  quality of asset, 29–30
  regulation, 32
  rental contract, type of, 30–2
  reversionary potential, 32
  tenant health, 32

232 INDEX

replacement value, 22–3
retail space, 24–5
return on invested capital (ROIC), 81, 82
  optimising, 83
returns, 3
reversionary potential/under-rented, 18, 32
  definition, 209
reversionary yield, 19
Reward per project, 112–13
Rich, Nigel, 219, 220
Rienecker, Maximilian, 182
risk management, 109
risk premium, 50
risk/reward profile of investment portfolio, 3–5
Ritblat, Jamie, 51–2, 83–4
Ritblat, Sir John, 65, 68–9, 217
Rock Investment, 95
Rodamco, 64
Rothschild, 68
Russia–Ukraine conflict, 72

S

S&P, 94
SBB, 147, 178–80
Schmid, Thilo, 191
SEGRO, 75, 78, 81, 219, 220, 222
Serra, Pere Viñolas, 221, 222
Shaftesbury Capital, 36
share buyback, 100–1
shareholder base, 159–60
  large shareholders, 159
  liquidity of shares, 159
  types of investors, 159–60
shareholder value destruction, 99–102
  boards, role of, 100
  governance and, 100
  return of capital, 100–1
Shurgard, 36
SIFF-Energies, 86
Signa, 36
Silicon Roundabout, 36
Simon Property Group, 94, 168, 175
Sirius Real Estate, 38, 83
Slade, Mike, 36, 39
Sleath, David, 222
Slough Estates, 78, 217, 219
  see also SEGRO
Smitsloo, Menno, 126
Société Générale, 86
St Modwen, 100

stock market rules, 193–201
  activism or company reportioning, 199
  benchmark investing, 200
  conservative guidance, 196
  conviction, 193
  daily clean sheet approach, 195
  equity market, lazy, 197
  insider trading and shareholder
    notifications, 201
  kitchen sinking, 196
  management teams, upset, 194–5
  one-minute convincing business case, 196
  optimism, 196
  proactivity, 194
  psychology of numbers and patterns, 198
  reversal patterns for similar companies, 199
  shared investment ideas, 197–8
  turning points, spotting, 194
  wish list, 195
Stockholm syndrome, 52, 166, 195
stocks in downturn, picking up, 197
Storage Stuff, 141
Sumner, Patrick, 75
supply, 22–5
supply/demand dynamics, 22–9
  supply, 22–5
  demand, 25–6
  direct market studies/models, 26–9
Sveafastigheter, 180
Swedish Financial Supervisory Authority, 180

T

TAG Immobilien, 72
Tallinn, Estonia, 25
taxation, 165
  Non-listed funds, 7
te Paske, Michiel, 17, 103
Templeton, Sir John, 44
tenant churn, 30
Thames River Capital, 167
theoretical ex-rights price (TERP), 143
TMT (Technology, Media and
    Telecoms) sector, 42
Tonckens, Jaap, 123, 128
total return, 17, 83
  definition, 209
TPG, 10, 144
TR Property Investment Trust, 167
Trafford Centre, Manchester, 168
TransAtlantic, 164

Index

transparency, 110
Tritant, Jean-Marie, 97
TSR (Total Shareholder Return), 113

U

UK Listing Authority, 75
UK REITs, 75, 76
Unibail-Rodamco, 52, 85–6, 91, 93–7, 219, 221
  see also Coeur Défense; URW
Unibail-Rodamco-Westfield *see* URW
URW, 52, 64, 94, 95–7, 111, 112
  REFOCUS plan, 95, 96
  RESET plan, 94, 95, 96
US REIT market, 157

V

valuation metrics, 128–31
valuation of portfolio, 131–2
value add potential, 35–8
  acquisitions and disposals, 37
  cluster or platform creation, 36
  property development, 36–7
  refurbishment, extension and
    alternative use, 35
  services, 37
value creation
  continuous, 81–97
  M&A (mergers and acquisitions), 90–7
value creators, 137–49
  accelerator effect, 147–9
  downward spiral
    fighting for survival, 138, 139, 146–7, 164
    stuck, 138, 139, 144–5
  stock selection, 148–9
  upward spiral
    firing on all cylinders, 138, 139–43,
      149, 164
    catalysts, 140
    right investment theme, 140
    strong value creation, 140
    unrealistic expectations, 142
    potential, 138, 139, 143, 144
value of global real estate, 1–2
van der Lubbe, Rutger, 125

van Garderen, Evert Jan, 30
Vastned Retail, 145–6
Verweij, Gijs, 64
Vetch, Nicholas, 139, 141
VGP NV, 143
Viceroy, 190, 191
Viguier, Jean-Paul, 85
Vonovia, 91–2, 188

W

Walcher, Guenther, 190, 191
Warburg, 68
Weighted Average Cost of Capital (WACC),
    49–51, 58, 81, 82
  optimising, 84–5
Wereldhave, 64
Westfield, 91, 93–7, 111
WeWork Inc., 43, 120
Whitehall Fund, 89
Whittaker, John, 166, 168
Wirecard, 186
Workspace, 220, 221

X

Xanadu shopping centre, Madrid, 170

Y

yield, 17–20, 48, 49
  asset, 19–20
  calculation of, 18–19
  definition, 209
  total return and, 17
yield compression, 66
  definition, 210
yield expansion, definition, 210
yield sensitivity, definition, 210
Young, 86

Z

Zell, Sam, 9
  Am I Being Too Subtle?, 44
Zig-Zag effect, 31–2
Zinnöcker, 191